4224

Department of Music Education
College of Music
Temple University

Y

PATG90-B6582

Learning to Conduct
and Rehearse

DANIEL L. KOHUT
Instrumental Music

JOE W. GRANT
Choral Music

School of Music, University of Illinois at Urbana-Champaign

PRENTICE HALL   Englewood Cliffs, New Jersey 07632

Library of Congress Cataloging-in-Publication Data

Kohut, Daniel L.
    Learning to conduct and rehearse / Daniel L. Kohut and
  Joe W. Grant.
        p.   cm.
    Includes bibliographical references.
    ISBN 0-13-526716-1
    1. Conducting. 2. Rehearsals (Music)   I. Grant, Joe W.
  II. Title.
  MT85.K683 1990
  781.45--dc20

                                            89-28018
                                               CIP
                                               MN

Editorial/production supervision and
  interior design: Arthur Maisel
Cover design: Miriam Recio
Manufacturing buyers: Mike Woerner
  and Carol Bystrom

© 1990 by Prentice-Hall, Inc.
A Division of Simon & Schuster
Englewood Cliffs, New Jersey 07632

Printed in the United States of America
10 9 8 7 6 5 4 3 2 1

ISBN   0-13-526716-1

Prentice-Hall International (UK) Limited, *London*
Prentice-Hall of Australia Pty. Limited, *Sydney*
Prentice-Hall Canada Inc., *Toronto*
Prentice-Hall Hispanoamericana, S.A., *Mexico*
Prentice-Hall of India Private Limited, *New Delhi*
Prentice-Hall of Japan, Inc., *Tokyo*
Simon & Schuster Asia Pte. Ltd., *Singapore*
Editora Prentice-Hall do Brasil, Ltda., *Rio de Janeiro*

Contents

8 *Rehearsal Procedures*

Index

Suggestions
for the Teacher

Teachers are afforded a great privilege—that of guiding and shaping the thoughts and actions of their students. This privilege is also accompanied by a grave responsibility—the teacher's duty of being as knowledgeable as possible regarding what is taught (content) and the proper way to present it (methodology). This section of the book deals mainly with the methodological aspects of the subject.

Although the title of this section indicates that it is for teachers rather than students, we hope that students will also read it. The more students know and the better they know it, the greater their potential for becoming fine conductors.

LEARNING SEQUENCE AND PACING PRINCIPLES

The logical way to learn any new skill is to begin with the simple and proceed gradually toward the complex. For example, as a first step toward learning how to walk, the human infant first learns to roll over in its crib. Then it learns to sit up, crawl, stand up, and finally walk. Eventually the child learns how to run and may even win some foot races, but the sequential order of skill acquisition outlined here is a fact of life. One doesn't learn how to run before first learning how to crawl and walk.

This process also takes considerable time, practice, and patience. Development of balance and coordination cannot be achieved overnight; it requires much trial-and-error practice. Patience is needed not only by the parents but also the child. One also needs to understand that making

x

errors when learning a new skill is natural and normal; it is an integral part of the learning process. Thus a combination of proper pacing and logical sequencing is all-important to efficient learning of new motor skills.

These principles apply equally to learning conducting skills. We need to begin with the very simple, most basic skills and work very gradually toward the ultimate goal of superior conducting and rehearsal ability. As teachers, we need to be sure that individual skills are introduced one at a time and in logical sequence. We also need to remind ourselves continually that considerable time, practice, and patience are required to achieve a high level of success.

This all sounds logical enough, and yet in the teaching of conducting this is often where the biggest errors are made. There is a tendency to "gloss over" fundamental skills, such as hand position and beat pattern clarity, and move on to the intermediate and advanced skills prematurely. There is also a strong tendency to expect the novice conductor to conduct musically, identify ensemble performance problems, and solve those problems quickly and efficiently—like an experienced conductor. But it cannot be done. The invariable result is extreme frustration for both student and teacher.

The main problem with this kind of instruction is mental overload. The student has too many things to think about and cannot concentrate on all of them at once. We need to remember that when learning new skills, human beings essentially operate with one-track minds. Considerable repetition is also required before new skills feel natural and easy. Once the natural and easy level is reached, something can be added.

Therefore, the first objective in working with beginning conductors is to teach the fundamentals of manual technique. Expressive, musical conducting is ultimately of prime importance, but focusing on it when one cannot yet give a good downbeat is "putting the cart before the horse." It can wait until later when the fundamentals of manual technique are secure. The same is even more true of rehearsal procedure. In fact the authors believe that rehearsal procedure should be delayed for most students until after they have reasonable control of the musical as well as mechanical aspects of baton technique. If introduced too soon some students will tend to rely primarily on their rehearsal ability to get performance results rather than achieving it through superior conducting technique. Primary emphasis should be focused on *showing* the performers via hand gestures, not *telling* them how with the mouth.

THE PSYCHOLOGY OF TEACHING CONDUCTING

Most students in a first semester conducting class will have reasonable proficiency on their major instrument or voice. This allows them to feel a measure of self-assurance as musicians. With regard to conducting, however, most of them will be absolute beginners—a condition that can be quite intimidating to some students. It is true that there are other classes like secondary instruments where one is also a beginner, but no one expects the students to be virtuosi on all of the instruments. With conducting, however, the situation is usually very different. Since most of the students enrolled are usually teachers in training, a significant portion of their professional life will be spent conducting and rehearsing large ensembles. For these students, conducting will become their primary musical asset, since it is often difficult to maintain performance facility later, when one is teaching full-time. Therefore, conducting is not just another course for these music students; it should be viewed as a second applied major subject, on the same level of importance as one's applied major instrument or voice.

Some may find this view rather shocking. How dare anyone suggest that another subject receive equal status to the applied music major! And yet the logic and practicality of such a view should be obvious to experienced teacher-conductors. All too often the study of conducting receives insufficient emphasis, with the result of graduates who have medicore manual technique and lack expressive ability. Such a situation is intolerable. Even the youngest choral and instrumental students deserve quality conducting and rehearsal technique from their teacher-conductors!

Nevertheless, attitudes change very slowly and musicians are perhaps even more conservative than most other professionals. Students sense this and getting them to spend enough time and effort in outside practice to achieve the needed level of proficiency is a challenge for even the best conducting teachers. But students can get motivation in many ways, including the inspiration of the teacher's own enthusiasm for conducting and his or her genuine concern for the students' progress. Yet the most powerful motivator (when judiciously used) ultimately may be the grades assigned by the teacher over the course of the semester.

For some students, however, motivation is not quite so simple. When the problem of beginning conductor intimidation is combined with lack of self-confidence, additional pressure from the teacher through tough grading seldom produces positive results. Such students need understanding, support, and encouragement from their teachers. Specific techniques which can be used are discussed in Kohut's *Musical Performance: Learning Theory and Pedagogy,* pages 43–50 and 135–141. Other recommended readings (listed alphabetically) are:

GALLWEY, W. TIMOTHY. *The Inner Game of Tennis.* New York: Random House, 1974.

GREEN, BARRY, with W. TIMOTHY GALLWEY. *The Inner Game of Music.* Garden City, NY: Anchor Press/Doubleday, 1986.

MALTZ, MAXWELL. *Psycho-Cybernetics.* New York: Pocket Books, 1960.

McGINNIS, ALAN LOY. *Bringing Out the Best in People.* Minneapolis: Augsburg Publishing House, 1985.

SUZUKI, SHINICHI. *Nurtured by Love.* New York: Exposition Press, 1969.

THE IMPORTANCE OF CONDUCTING A LIVE ENSEMBLE

One approach to the teaching of conducting is to have students practice with recordings. Recordings are fine when used as a part of score study and for listening to other conductors' interpretations. When used as a primary means for learning manual technique, they are of limited value.

Among the main problems with practicing to a recording is that there is no way one can *lead* the performers; all one can do is *follow* them. Conducting students desperately need to experience performer response (or the lack of it) to their gestures. An even greater problem with recordings is that they provide no opportunity for developing leadership ability. Since leadership is probably *the* most important qualification needed by the conductor, this is a serious consequence. Therefore, to really learn to conduct, the authors believe that students should work with live musicians—at least a trio or quartet.

We recognize that setting up a full orchestra, band, or choir solely for laboratory conducting purposes is not practical in most situations. But it is also not the only solution to the problem. Every conducting student is usually a performer on some instrument or voice. Thus in every conducting class there will surely be at least one trio or quartet that can be formed. In the beginning stages of learning, this size of ensemble is all that is needed. In fact instrumental conductors are usually better off dealing with only three or four parts at first, rather than a full band or orchestra score of twenty or more staves.

Even so, there is still the problem of finding suitable literature. Ideally the literature used should be sequenced so that it proceeds gradually from the very simple toward the more complex with respect to conducting technique. Solving this problem is challenging enough. Trying to solve it in the context of finding literature for the specific small ensemble combinations available in your class will likely be next to impossible. We have solved the problem for you in Part II of this text by providing musical excerpts, selected and sequenced to meet the needs of beginning and intermediate level conductors. These excerpts, all scored in concert pitch, require players of transposing instruments to do their own transposition. While this may present a few difficulties for some players at first, experience has shown that these soon disappear.

USE OF VIDEOTAPE AS A TEACHING-LEARNING TOOL

Psychologists tell us that one of the things that we do poorest is self-evaluation. The reason for this is that we do not see ourselves the way others see us. Naturally, this also applies to our conducting and rehearsal behaviors—that is, unless we are able to see ourselves on videotape.

We consider videotape feedback to be so valuable that we use it every time student conductors rehearse and conduct in class. We also recommend that, to the extent possible, conducting teachers meet with each student for a brief conference periodically to view the tape together. At the very least, provisions should be made for the students to view their own videotapes alone. Eventually, students need to learn how to teach themselves. A major objective of conferences with the instructor should be showing the students how to accomplish this.

1 *Manual Technique Fundamentals*

The content and organization of this chapter and Chapter Two are based on two pedagogical premises: (1) that there are specific fundamentals of conducting that should be isolated and studied first; and (2) that there is a logical sequence in which these fundamentals should be introduced for optimum learning efficiency. The fundamentals to be covered in this first chapter are pivot points and planes of motion, proper stance, ready position, the initial preparatory and ictus motions, the preparatory-downbeat sequence, and the cutoff.

PRELIMINARY CONSIDERATIONS

What is music? What is conducting? What is the purpose of conducting? These items are so basic that the reader may wonder why we bothered to include them. Yet the fact that they are so very basic is precisely the reason we believe that it would be a mistake to omit them.

What Is Music?

Music is sound and silence aesthetically organized in time. Of special importance to conductors is the fact that music is also a nonverbal form of artistic expression. As such it cannot be easily or effectively described in words. This means that during rehearsal conductors should communicate their musical concepts and ideas mainly through nonverbal means: conducting gestures and the singing voice. Excessive verbal description is inappropriate and inefficient and should therefore be avoided.

1

2

What Is Conducting?

Conducting is musical sign language. It is a visual representation of the conductor's musical ear. Put in another way, conducting means communication. The conductor communicates musical ideas visually to the ensemble via hand gestures and facial expressions. Conducting is also a perceptual-motor skill, one which must be practiced carefully and diligently to be learned properly. At its highest level conducting is an art. A conductor's gestures are a "musical trademark" at least as personal as that of a first-rank virtuoso performer.

As musicians, we have all heard about (and probably observed) the sort of conductors commonly referred to as "showmen," persons whose gestures are overdone for show alone. Showmen can usually get away with visual gymnastics when in front of a superior professional ensemble; in fact most professional ensembles are capable of performing adequately, much of the time, without a conductor. Less-skilled musicians, on the other hand, need clean, clear gestures and guidance from a conductor; they do not need a showman. Actually, there is no room for showmanship by conductors at any level, in our opinion. Most professional musicians will agree. So do not make the mistake of trying to emulate a showman; strive to be very clear and efficient in your gestures. Communicate through economy of means, not excess motion.

The Role and Function of the Conductor

Before learning how to do anything, it is worth examining why we propose to learn it. What is the role of the conductor? What function does this individual serve? Before these questions can be answered, we first need to know with what level of ensemble the conductor will be working, and in what setting. Will it be a professional group, community orchestra, church choir, or municipal band? Will it be in an academic setting, and at what level: college, high school, or elementary?

Clearly, the role and function of the professional conductor at one extreme is quite different from that of the elementary school teacher/ conductor at the other. The professional conductor's primary mission is to prepare music for public performance. Having professional musicians at one's disposal means that rehearsal time will be devoted largely to style, interpretation, balance, and other nontechnical aspects of performance. In the case of school ensembles, however, the performers will not be masters of their instruments or their voices, and will need help with technique. They will also need help with music fundamentals like pitch and rhythm, and their teacher/conductor must be prepared to provide that kind of help. At the elementary school level, one must also be able literally to teach the students *how* to play their instruments in ensemble and *how* to sing properly. Methods and materials for teaching music reading and sight singing are also needed by teacher/conductors working with school ensembles.

Despite the differences, a primary function of all conductors is to recreate in sound and silence the expressive qualities of the musical symbols and ideas created and notated by the composer. This requires a wide variety of personal and musical skills. It also requires fluency in the basic fundamentals of conducting, which is the main focus of this and the next chapter.

INITIAL STEPS

Conducting technique, like vocal and instrumental performance technique, should be a means to an end, not an end in itself. It should be based on logical and justifiable principles related to the musical, physiological, psychological, and visual concepts of the conducting art. Every movement of the hands and every facial expression should serve a practical or musical function; every action should make a positive difference in the ensemble's performance. Those movements and actions that fail to meet these goals are superfluous and should be eliminated. The purpose of conducting technique, therefore, is to help the conductor realize musical goals in the most efficient and effective manner. In this connection we recommend that two primary items be kept in mind:

1. The best approach for learning most new skills is to concentrate on doing things in the most natural way. The most natural way is usually the best way because it is the most relaxed way. Excessive tension ruins technique in conducting the same as it does in singing or instrumental performance. Undue stiffness in the fingers, hands, or arms (except for certain special functions) should therefore be avoided.

2. Acquisition of conducting technique requires mastery of numerous individual skills. These skills should be practiced separately away from the music until they become second nature and can be done without conscious concentration, like riding a bicycle or driving a car.

The skills described below are to be practiced separately in front of a mirror. Later, go from one directly to the other without stopping in between. Always watch for clarity of gesture, economy of means, and relaxed, smooth movements characteristic of a good athlete. All conducting at this time should also be done with the hands alone (no baton) in order to promote good, relaxed wrist and arm movement.

Pivot Points and Planes of Motion

RANGE-OF-MOTION EXERCISES. Since conducting is a physical activity, we need to become acquainted first with the functions of those body parts that are used in the conducting process. Flexibility and freedom of movement are essential in good conducting technique. These functions should be introduced via the "conducting pivot points" which are the natural pivot points of the shoulder, elbow, wrist, hand, and fingers.

In the same way that an actor or a mime explores the use of facial

4

expressions, body posture, and gesture, conductors should investigate the range of motions possible at each pivot point. Isolate your sense of feeling and kinesthetic awareness and focus on each of the pivot points, one at a time. Begin with the shoulder joint. Without moving the elbow and wrist, allow the shoulder to pivot freely as the arm is lifted from your side. Rotate it to the front of the body, then swing it in a wide circle from front to back. Move it in as many directions as it will swing comfortably without tension.

Next explore the motions possible with the elbow pivot. Let your arms hang freely at your sides. Concentrate on each pivot point and make sure each is relaxed. Now lift only your forearms, bending at the elbow joints. Explore the motions of up, down, left and right that can be made while the upper arms continue to hang at your sides. Try lifting the upper arms until they are parallel to the floor and swing the forearms in as many directions as they will move.

To free the wrists of tension, shake the arms vigorously while bending over at the waist. Allow each of the joints to flop about. Now stand upright, raise the hands to shoulder level and let the wrists flop in the same fashion. Make sure to let the hands move from side to side as well as up and down. This side-to-side flexibility will be extremely important in executing the legato gesture.

Now explore the motions and shapes that can be created with the hands and fingers. Open them to a stiff, flat position; close them into fists; curve them slowly into arcs and curls; open and close your fingers; then combine all of these movements with a variety of wrist positions.

Finally, combine all of the pivot points in a free-swinging exploration of all the possible movements and contortions that the various joints will allow. Focus on the freedom and flexibility at each point. If tension is felt, take time to "shake loose" in that isolated joint, then get back into the flowing motions with the whole arm, shoulder, elbow, wrist, and hand.

This may seem like a futile exercise in less-than-creative movement. It is not. In class, the range-of-motion exercises should be done with a positive attitude, encouragement, and a strong dose of humor. They are effective ways to identify and get in touch with the kinesthetic sensations of freedom and flexibility needed to conduct in an effortless, tension-free manner. The exercises also act as a good "ice-breaker" for the class members. Everyone looks pretty silly doing them, and the inhibitions of "How will I *look* conducting in front of everyone?" are reduced through these free-form motion exercises.

As you do the range-of-motion exercises be aware of the planes of motion through which your arms, hands, and wrists are moving. The vertical, horizontal, and diagonal planes, as well as the distance to and away from the body, are the space in which the conducting gestures will be made. Close your eyes (to heighten your kinesthetic sense) and move through each of the planes using each of the pivot points. Move the full arm through each plane, forearms only, pivoting first with the elbow and then the hands and wrists. Keep the pivot points free and flexible as you explore as many shapes and motions as the joints will comfortably allow.

Proper Stance

Stand with the head and upper body erect and the feet apart, approximately the width of the shoulders, and one foot (usually the left) slightly forward of the other. The goal is to establish good posture and body balance in order to prevent excessive muscular tension, especially in the large muscles of the legs, shoulders, upper back, and neck areas. Dropping the head downward, slumping over at the waist, slouching on one leg—all of these are examples of poor posture to be avoided.

A word of caution. . . . It is all too easy to read quickly through this section and the one following, and digest very little of either. To avoid this we recommend that you read and re-read these sections slowly and carefully since they deal with the very foundation of good conducting technique. Excessive tension in the arms or shoulders due to poor body balance, and beat patterns with the elbows too low or high are the most common problems of beginner conductors. Avoid the need for time-consuming remedial work later by getting the basics right the first time.

Ready Position of the Arms, Hands, and Fingers

1. Begin by letting your arms hang loosely at your sides and hold your hands in a relaxed position with the thumbs and fingers curved inward naturally. The goal is to relax the arms and hands as much as possible.

2. Next lift both arms upward while simultaneously moving the elbows outward and forward so that the forearms are *almost* parallel to the floor and also in line horizontally with the solar plexis (the place in the center of the chest where the ribs divide) as shown in Photograph 1.

   When lifting the arms and elbows, concentrate on using just enough energy to execute the task and no more. Using too many muscles results in excessive tension which often localizes itself in the shoulders. Tension ruins technique.

3. Check to see that the palms of both hands are *almost* parallel to the floor as in Photograph 2. If they are not, lift the elbows until they are. Do not try to get the palms down by twisting the forearms inward as in Photograph 3. This is unnatural and thus incorrect because it creates excessive tension in both the arms and the wrists.

4. Note in Photograph 2 that both hands are in line vertically with their respective shoulders. Check to see that your hands are similarly positioned. This has a direct impact on placement of the beat frame (to be discussed later in this chapter).

5. The position of the arms and elbows described thus far is equivalent to where the downbeat will be. To reinforce (and double check) correct forearm and elbow height, move your forearms inward horizontally until both hands touch the solar plexis area. Then swing the forearms outward

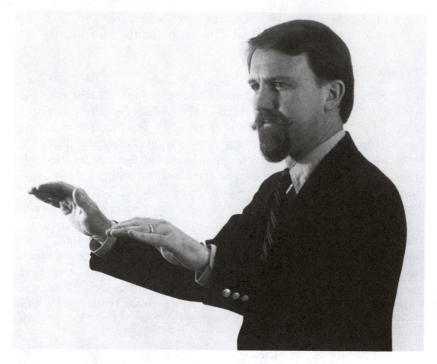

PHOTOGRAPH 1.

until the hands are in line with their respective shoulders. Move the forearms slowly in and out like this several times. Watch yourself in a mirror at first; then practice with your eyes closed for kinesthetic reinforcement. The eventual goal is to be fully aware of where your arms are in terms of position and space without the need for visual feedback.

PHOTOGRAPH 2.   Correct

PHOTOGRAPH 3.   Incorrect

6. Now focus on the position of the fingers. Up to this point you have been asked to keep the fingers in a normal relaxed position with the thumbs and fingers curved inward naturally. Now this needs to be changed, because this finger position will not provide a clear point to the beat. If all of the fingers are raised at the knuckle joints and extended as if ready for a firm hand shake, this creates a point of focus (tip of the second finger) in the same way that the tip of a baton creates a point of focus (see Photograph 4 below).

In assuming the new finger position be careful that the fingers are not held straight out: This causes excessive tension which quickly radiates to the wrists. Also avoid having the thumbs stick out. This usually causes the fingers to spread apart too far which also creates excessive tension.

Again double check to see that the palms face downward. If they face inward, this will result in improper wrist action and poor movement flexibility. Lift the elbows until the palms face downward.

Extreme elbow positions that are either too low or too high constitute one of the greatest problems experienced by young conductors. Instrumental conductors standing on a podium looking down at players who are seated tend to drop the elbows and lower the beat frame excessively. Choral conductors, on the other hand, tend to look up at singers who are standing on risers and lift the elbows and the beat frame excessively. Both extremes should be avoided. Care should be taken from the very beginning to see that elbow height is in an acceptable range.

PHOTOGRAPH 4.

The Preparatory and Downbeat Motions

To give a downbeat means executing the entire movement shown in Diagrams 1 and 2. The preparatory beat consists of the initial preparatory motion and the movement toward the downbeat ictus. The downbeat follows without pause as the hand changes direction and moves toward the ictus. The initial preparatory motion defines the beginning of the preparatory beat. The icus defines the point in time that the beat actually occurs. In Diagrams 1 and 2 the ictus shown is the downbeat ictus or attack.

The first function of the preparatory and downbeat motions is to allow the ensemble to make a simultaneous entrance on the first sound of the piece. Two styles of preparatory beats are shown below. In our opinion, the style shown in Diagram 1 will insure better ensemble attacks because the beginning of the preparatory beat and the downbeat ictus are essentially in the same place. The plane of the ictus is established by the plane of the initial preparatory motion. In Diagram 2 this is not the case. The downbeat could come almost anywhere on its downward descent. Nevertheless, there are fine conductors who use this style and your instructor may prefer that you also use it.

Because correct execution of the preparatory and downbeat motions is so important, we will study and practice its parts in detail before attempting the complete preparatory-downbeat sequence.

The initial preparatory motion involves an *upward* snap of the hands at the wrists. The ictus involves a *downward* snap of the hands at the wrists. The initial preparatory movement is a very gentle action while the ictus is usually heavier and more pronounced. Those who have studied snare drum may wish to think of the initial preparatory motion as being similar to the "up tap" of a snare drum stick. The ictus motion, on the other hand, feels like the "down tap" of a snare drum stick. Since these movements cannot be easily described in words, they are best learned by observing and imitating your instructor.

It is very important that the above movements be executed with a snap of the *wrists*, not by using the forearms. Some conductors, especially when using a baton, create their icti by "bouncing" the entire forearm while the wrist remains stationary. This signals a heavy marcato style to

DIAGRAM 1

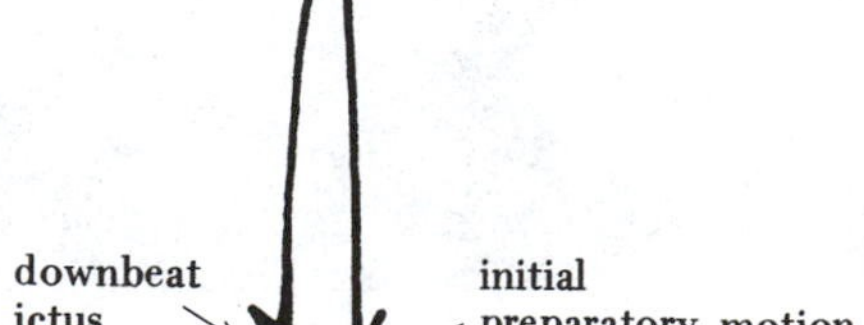

downbeat
ictus

initial
preparatory motion

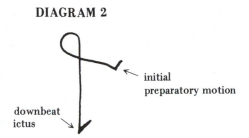

the performers. The icti in legato, staccato, and even lighter forms of marcato, should be executed with the wrist, not the forearm.

In order for the motions to be done properly, the palms of the hands should face downward toward the floor. This allows the wrist joints to function in their most natural and efficient way, with the hands moving straight up and down. If the palms do not face downward, lift the elbows until they do.

Executing an ictus with the palms of the hands facing each other is possible but the range of motion is greatly restricted. It is also very inefficient because it makes additional motion necessary: Both the hands and forearms must twist sideways in order to execute a downward motion. In this respect we ask that you consider the hand position of the pianist and timpanist. Both have the palms down for the same reason as a good conductor—so that the wrists can move up and down as easily and efficiently as possible.

Slowly practice a series of initial preparatory motions. Concentrate on *lifting* the hands and forearms upward. Think also of pulling your hands away from a *warm* stove. We say warm rather than hot stove because the motion should be gentle, not frantic. All you want is to indicate clearly when and where the preparatory beat begins.

Next, practice a series of ictus motions. Practice very slowly and concentrate on a downward snap of the hands. Think of throwing a small object like a ball toward the floor.

The ictus motion is used to define every beat in a measure, of course, not just the downbeat. Every ictus should have a downward feeling except the last beat in the measure where an upward lifting motion feels more appropriate.

Finally, practice one initial preparatory motion followed by one ictus motion. Continue alternating slowly between the two until they both feel reasonably natural and easy. Once this happens you are ready to try the complete preparatory-downbeat sequence.

The Preparatory-Downbeat Sequence

Before practicing the actual preparatory-downbeat sequence, first establish an authoritative stance and make direct eye contact with your ensemble. Do this by bringing your arms up to ready position, standing

10

still and looking at everyone in the ensemble. This will help you make sure that everyone is ready and concentrating so that a good attack is possible. This is also the time when you need to assert yourself visually as the leader of your ensemble.

With the arms, hands, and fingers in the correct ready position, execute the preparatory beat up to about eye level and then, without any stopping or slowing down, return to the original starting place and execute the ictus. After execution of the ictus, all movement should stop for now (see Diagram 3).

When all movement stops after the downbeat ictus as requested above, the response of an ensemble will be to perform a short note; i.e., when the conductor's hands stop, the tone stops. Herein lies a basic principle of conducting: To continue the tone as in a fermata, keep the hands moving; otherwise the tone will stop as if it were marked staccato.

In executing the preparatory beat, be careful not to stop or hesitate in any way at the top of the movement cycle. This creates special performance problems for singers and wind players which will be discussed on page 12. In fact any kind of hesitancy or evidence of insecurity will invariably result in a poor ensemble attack on the downbeat. Concentrate on the preparatory beat being one continuous up and down movement. Act as though you know what you are doing and give the downbeat with assurance.

It is also a good idea for the conductor to breathe with the singers or players. Open the mouth and inhale at the very beginning of the preparatory beat; exhale right on the downbeat. This helps insure that everyone is thinking and functioning together.

In the case of wind players who need extra drill in this area, the conductor should have them whisper "oh" while inhaling during the preparatory beat, and whisper "toh" on the downbeat. Do a series of these whisper drills until they are done correctly (oh-toh, oh-toh, oh-toh, etc.). Then have them do the same thing several times with instruments.

When conducting singers the conductor may want to inhale on "oh" and mouth the first word of the phrase to be sung. Mouthing is allowed for the first word only, however. We believe that continual mouthing of the words or even singing with the ensemble interferes with both the conductor's hearing and conducting. The conductor cannot possibly hear as

DIAGRAM 3

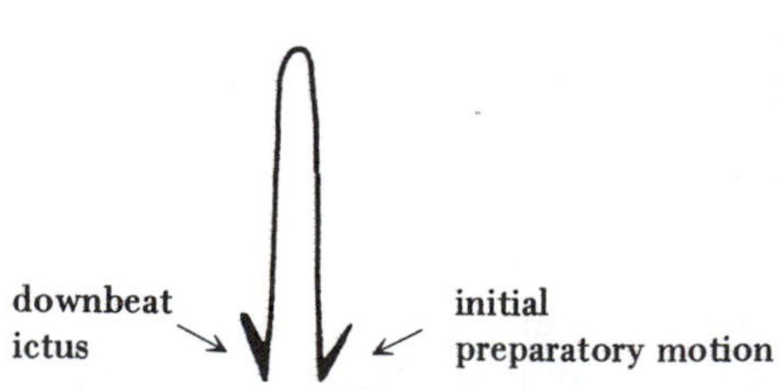

downbeat ictus → → ← initial preparatory motion

well if concentrating on singing. The conducting is further compromised by the fact that the performers learn to watch the conductor's mouth almost entirely instead of the hands. In polyphonic music with independent voice lines and texts, conductor singing/mouthing is especially confusing.

Now practice doing the complete preparatory-downbeat sequence several times slowly until the movement itself feels reasonably comfortable. Then, while silently counting a measure of slow $\frac{4}{4}$ meter to yourself, start the preparatory beat on count four and let the downbeat fall on the count of one. Concentrate on giving a clear initial preparatory motion and then moving decisively toward a firm downbeat. Do not be hesitant in any way.

The main function of the preparatory beat is to get the ensemble in on time for the downbeat. In addition, the preparatory beat should convey three other items of information: the tempo, dynamic level, and style (legato, marcato, or staccato) of the first note. We recommend that the preparatory-downbeat sequence be practiced in various tempi, dynamic levels, and styles until all feel comfortable. For example, practice counting one measure of a slow, legato four-beat meter to yourself and give a gentle pianissimo downbeat. Count one measure of a fast marcato three-beat meter and give a heavy forte downbeat. Create other practice combinations for yourself. In this way, from the very beginning, you can concentrate on making your movements musical, not mechanical.

At this point, take some time to review and work on all of the following in front of a full length mirror. After item 1 feels comfortable, add item 2, then item 3, and item 4.

1. With your arms in ready position, establish an authoritative stance and direct eye contact with your imaginary ensemble.

2. Do the complete preparatory-downbeat sequence. Get comfortable with the feel of a good initial preparatory motion, continuous movement toward the downbeat, and a clear, definite ictus. Practice with your eyes open looking into the mirror. Also practice with your eyes closed and concentrate on the kinesthetic sensations of this movement sequence.

3. Now practice breathing while doing the preparatory-downbeat sequences. Practice "oh-toh."

4. Finally, practice the preparatory-downbeat sequence using a variety of tempi, dynamic levels, and musical styles.

After practicing alone, the entire sequence should be performed with live musicians in class. Direct feedback is the only real way to determine if one's gestures are clear and definite. Be very conscious at this time of looking each of your performers in the eye while in the ready position. This is phase one of leadership on the podium and has at least as much to do with the quality of the ensemble attack as proper movement of the hands.

The preparatory-downbeat sequence is the most basic technical skill a conductor possesses. It should be executed easily and naturally before going ahead. It should also be practiced several times daily to instill its proper execution. Resist all temptations to move ahead prematurely.

Causes of Poor Attacks

The importance of correct hand movements and corresponding inhalation and attack responses from the performers during the preparatory-downbeat sequence cannot be overemphasized. Every good conductor understands this: it is the reason why significant attention is traditionally given to this fundamental in rehearsal. However, much precious time is often wasted when improper or confusing procedures are employed. One of these is when the conductor slows down hand movement at the top of the preparatory beat before coming back down. Beginning conductors may even stop hand movement completely at the top of the gesture. This causes many singers and wind players instinctively to stop inhaling and to hold their breath until the downbeat. Holding the air back requires unnatural tensing of the expiratory muscles. This in turn induces excessive tension throughout the tone production mechanism, especially the glottis and the throat area. The result is consistently poor downbeat attacks.

As stated earlier, the movement from the beginning of the preparatory beat through the downbeat should be continuous. Likewise the breathing sequence for the conductor, singers, and wind players should be continuous, in direct correlation with the conductor's hand movements. Inhalation should commence at the very beginning of the preparatory beat and continue without interruption until the instant just before the downbeat. The conductor's opening his or her mouth and breathing along with the performers can do much to help insure good breathing and correct hand movements resulting in good attacks.

An even greater problem exists when the conductor asks the singers or wind players to "get set" ahead of time by inhaling a big breath *before* the beginning of the preparatory gesture. The intent may be meritorious but the result is usually disappointing. The problem is the same as when the conductor stops hand movement at the top of the preparatory beat, only worse. Inhaling and holding the breath before the preparatory gesture induces greater tension due to holding the breath longer. Inhale *during* the entire preparatory beat, not before.

The Cutoff

Do the preparatory-downbeat sequence but this time do not stop hand movement after the downbeat. Instead, immediately after the ictus move both hands horizontally away from each other as shown in Diagram 4. This movement indicates that you want the tone to continue.

To stop the tone, give the loop-type cutoff shown in Diagram 4 above. Note that a small outward stopping motion is needed after forming the loop to indicate the precise moment of the release.

DIAGRAM 4

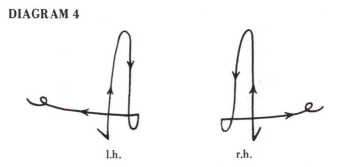

l.h.   r.h.

You are now able to start and stop your ensemble and control the length of the sound produced in between. Using any pitch or chord of your choice, conduct the fermatas shown in Example 1. Be sure to establish good eye contact before giving the preparatory beats.

Legato attacks and releases should be light and gentle. In contrast, marcato attacks should be heavy and the releases rather abrupt and strong. Listen to the ensemble: the style and loudness of their performance will tell you how effective your gestures are.

The loop-type cutoff shown in Diagram 4 is recommended for all of the fermatas in Example 1. The ''check mark'' or phrase ending release will be covered in Chapter 2.

Practice Procedures

Conducting is a skill. Acquiring this skill requires conscientious daily practice. The following summary of conducting basics is included to assist you in organizing your practice sessions. All are to be practiced in front of a full length mirror.

STANCE.   Check the position of your feet in relation to each other—the distance between them and your posture in general. The goal is to achieve positive control of the body musculature through good posture and body balance.

READY POSITION.   Bring both arms upward easily and naturally so that they are almost parallel to the floor. Check to see that the elbows are away from the sides and forward of the body. Are the palms of the hands down?

EXAMPLE I.   Fermata practice exercise

Short soft
fermata

Long loud
fermata

Soft legato attack
and release

Loud marcato attack
and release

*This is the cesura symbol which means to stop the tone completely (complete cutoff) before going on to the next note. A new preparatory beat should also be used to start each new fermata.

14

Are the fingers raised at the knuckles so that they can provide a good point to the beat? Do not forget that the hands should be in line with their respective shoulders. Repeat this process several times before going ahead.

In preparation for giving the downbeat, be sure to assume an authoritative stance and establish direct eye contact with all of the performers. Avoid looking straight ahead only; glance also to both sides.

THE INITIAL PREPARATORY AND ICTUS MOTIONS. With both arms in ready position, perform a series of initial preparatory motions using a gentle upward snap of the hands. Then do a series of icti with a downward snap of the hands. Check to see that the palms of the hands are down so that the wrists can move up and down easily and naturally. Think "up tap" for the initial preparatory motions; think "down tap" for the icti motions.

THE PREPARATORY-DOWNBEAT SEQUENCE. With both arms in ready position, begin the preparatory beat, lift the arms to about eye level, and without stopping or hesitating move directly into the downbeat ictus. Practice breathing during the sequence. Whisper "oh-toh," and always precede each preparatory beat by first establishing direct eye contact with the ensemble.

THE CUTOFF. Finally, add the cutoff to the above. Practice doing all of the fermatas included in Example 1 on page 13. Be sure to keep both hands moving during each fermata and move the hands horizontally, not vertically. Vertical hand movement indicates crescendo.

MENTAL IMAGERY. A method that has proven successful in mastering skills like conducting is that of mental imagery. In using this method, first create a very detailed mental picture of the action about to take place before it is executed. The golfer, for example, imagines making the perfect swing, "feels" the contact with the ball, "watches" it in flight, and "sees" it land on the green near the flag.

To use this method with conducting, imagine yourself in front of an ensemble as a professional conductor. Mentally picture yourself checking to make sure the group is prepared, lifting your arms to the ready position, and executing a perfect preparatory-downbeat sequence. Allow yourself to "hear" the sound that your group makes in response to your gesture. Now "rewind the tape" of this image and watch it again. After several "viewings" practice the gesture yourself, noticing how you feel as you do the gesture. Do you look and feel like the mental image that you imagined? Relax and let your body recreate the images that you observed in your imagination.

For this technique to be effective, lots of stored images of good conducting are needed. These can only be gained by watching and noticing the detailed actions of outstanding conductors. This should include modeling of your conducting teacher as well as attending concerts and rehearsals of professional conductors whenever possible.

REINFORCING KINESTHETIC SENSATION. Conducting is a perceptual-motor skill. It is perceptual in that one must have a clear mental image of the musical ideas one intends to express via hand gestures before actually doing them. The motor aspect involves actual arm movements which are external and thus readily observed. It also involves internal function called kinesthesis which cannot be observed visually but is equally important to skill learning and habit formation. Some refer to it as "muscle memory." It is that certain indescribable feeling we experience in all motor activities.

When we execute a given movement, the brain makes a recording of the kinesthetic sensation we experienced. With repetition, the kinesthetic recordings are reinforced automatically, assuming we execute the movement in the same way each time. But to reinforce kinesthetic sensations still more effectively, some of our practice should be done with the eyes closed.

Let us explain specifically what we mean. When both of the arms are brought up to the ready position in front of a mirror, check to see if they are almost parallel to the floor. Drop the hands at your sides and repeat the process several times until it feels natural to bring the arms into correct position without undue concentration. Then close your eyes, concentrate on kinesthetic sensation (how it is supposed to feel), and bring the arms into position several times. Check yourself periodically by opening your eyes to see if your arms are in the correct position. If incorrect, go back and do several repetitions with the eyes open. Then close the eyes again and concentrate on kinesthetic sensation alone. (Incidentally, what we are trying to develop here is the same kind of ability required to play the piano without watching the fingers.)

Focusing on kinesthetic sensation is important in yet another critical area: avoiding excessive muscular tension. As a first step to recognizing this problem, make as tight a fist as you can in both hands and tense both arms as much as you can. Maintain this tension while you count to four slowly. Then relax immediately and count to four, then tense for four counts, then relax. . . . Now bring the arms up to the ready position using just enough energy to accomplish this task but no more. Achieving the goal of a tension-free musculature allows you to execute the preparatory-downbeat-cutoff sequence more easily, naturally, and efficiently. If there is excessive tension in the arms, the movements will invariably be awkward and robot-like.

A common problem is that the muscles may be quite tense but you simply do not realize it. One way to check yourself for excessive tension in the ready position is to bring the arms into ready position, then relax them completely and instantaneously so that they drop quickly at your sides. If they do not drop quickly, this indicates excessive arm tension; too many muscles are being used to bring the arms into position and to hold them there. To solve this problem, practice bringing the arms into position (concentrating on minimal energy) and then dropping them quickly at your sides. Repeat this several times as needed.

With students who experience severe difficulties with tension, we recommend that instructor and student face each other with their arms at ready position. The instructor takes hold of both of the student's hands and asks the student to relax both arms completely and totally, perhaps even shaking the student's arms to help achieve total relaxation. Then, without any warning to the student, the instructor lets go of the student's hands. If the arms drop quickly, they are relaxed; if they drop slowly, there is excessive tension.

The initial basics of stance, ready position, plus the preparatory-downbeat-cutoff sequence should be done reasonably well (without the presence of excessive tension) before going ahead to the next section. Proceeding prematurely will only create the need for remedial work later.

CONCLUSION.   In approaching the study and practice of conducting, realize that becoming a fine conductor with good manual technique and superior interpretive ability is no less a challenge than that of becoming a virtuoso performer. In areas such as score study and rehearsal procedure, the demands are especially great. This obviously means lots of concentrated individual practice is required in order to achieve any level of success. How you, the conducting student, approach your practice is even more important than *how much* you practice. Below are three basic guidelines designed to help you get the most out of your practice sessions.

1. Practice in front of a full length mirror and work on one thing at a time. Do each individual skill several times until it feels reasonably natural before moving on to the next.
2. Practice slowly, especially at the beginning of your practice session. Some of the practice should be done in super slow motion.
3. Several short practice sessions each day are usually far more productive than one or two long ones. When physical practice is not possible or practical, practice your conducting skills mentally. Picture yourself doing each skill perfectly.

Using a Podium and Risers

The purpose of podiums and risers is to help the performers see the conductor and his or her gestures more easily. In most choral ensembles this is achieved best through risers alone. A podium usually is not necessary. With bands and orchestras a podium is needed and is used in most situations. With very large instrumental ensembles, risers are often used in the back rows as an additional aid in seeing the conductor.

The podium also emphasizes the conductor's role of authority. When a conductor steps on the podium, experienced musicians know that all talking should stop and full attention should be given up front. In other words, the conductor is ready to begin. For this reason some choral conductors also like to use a podium.

Should a podium be used when conducting small ensembles (or a conducting class) of up to twenty performers? The answer depends upon the height of the conductor. Conductors who are very short will need to use a podium even with small groups. Otherwise their beat pattern will not be seen easily unless they raise it excessively. Conductors of medium height and taller, however, should refrain from using a podium in such circumstances. Doing so usually results in the beat pattern dropping lower and lower until it is around waist level or below. The bottom of the beat pattern should be in line with the solar plexis (place where the ribs divide).

Position of the Conductor's Stand

The conductor's stand should be positioned low enough so that the conductor's entire beat frame is clearly visible to the performers at all times. To adjust the stand for proper height, stand up straight with the left arm held straight down with the palm of the hand resting flat on top of the score. If it is necessary to bend down to position the hand correctly, the stand is too low. If it is necessary to bend the left arm at the elbow to get the palm of the hand in place, then the stand is too high. Both the body and arm should be perfectly straight. If a podium is used, adjustment of stand height should be made while standing on the podium, of course.

2 Standard Conducting Gestures

Now that you know how to start and stop an ensemble, the next step is to learn the standard gestures used in between the downbeat and the cutoff. Toward this end the following topics will be covered: the basic four-, three-, two-, and one-beat patterns; indicating tempo, dynamics, and musical style; using the baton; and left hand techniques.

THE BASIC FOUR-, THREE-, TWO-, AND ONE-BEAT PATTERNS

Every ensemble musician has seen the four, three, two, and one patterns so many times that detailed discussion of the same here may seem unnecessary. Why not simply include a chart of all of the beat pattern diagrams and get on to the next topic? Actually there is far more to this topic than one might imagine. Clear, accurate beat patterns are as important to good conducting as correct breathing is to wind playing and singing, efficient bow control is to string playing, and correct stick technique is to percussion playing. Beat patterns should clearly indicate not only the number of beats in a measure but many other important elements as well. Beat patterns are basic skills that need to be practiced daily.

The first problem beginning conductors often have with beat patterns is remembering which way to move on beat two. Example 2 answers the question. Note that in the three pattern, beat two is to the conductor's right. In the four pattern, beat two is to the conductor's left.

Up to this point all of the gestures have involved both arms, each one mirroring the actions of the other. In learning the beat patterns, how-

EXAMPLE 2.   *two pattern   = down   up*
                    three pattern = down   right   up
                    four pattern   = down   left   right   up

ever, we recommend that only the right arm be used. The left arm is to be used mainly to start and stop the ensemble, and for cuing, accents, dynamic changes, and other special purposes. It should definitely not be used continually to mirror the beat pattern of the right arm. If so used, it loses most of its special function.

When not in use, the left hand should be in a "neutral position" at the waist or resting at the side. Some conductors feel most comfortable holding it against the left side of the chest (against the coat lapel).

We recommend use of the right hand only for conducting beat patterns, even if you are left-handed. A variety of reasons have been given over the years why the left hand should not be used for this purpose, including the argument that ensemble performers will be confused when trying to respond to a left-handed beat pattern. Whether or not this is really true is secondary. The essential factor is that left-handed conducting is not accepted by the music profession as a whole. Conductors who persist in conducting left-handed need to realize that they will probably have to justify it repeatedly to other musicians for the rest of their lives.

Some readers who are left-handed may feel that the authors do not really understand, that they are insensitive to left-handed people who must deal with discrimination daily in what is primarily a right-hand-oriented society. To put this thought to rest let it be known that one of the authors is left-handed yet learned to conduct with no severe difficulties with the right hand. It really isn't that difficult!

Before delving into a discussion of the beat patterns themselves, the beat frame (area where the beat pattern is placed) and the concept of primary and secondary metric accents will be discussed.

Position of the Beat Frame

The bottom of the beat frame should be in line horizontally with the solar plexis. The top of the beat frame should be at about eye level. Keeping the beat frame within these boundaries allows the performers to see the conductor's eyes, facial expressions, and conducting gestures simultaneously. The performers should be able to look up from the music and quickly see a framed "snapshot" of both the beat pattern and the conductor's face. Still another way to conceptualize this is too think of a well-framed video or television picture which includes all of the needed arm and facial information (see Photograph 5). If the pattern is too far off to the right as in Photograph 6, the conductor's face will be "out of the picture."

Also note in Photograph 5 that the vertical center of the beat frame is in line with the right shoulder. This is as it should be logically since the downbeat is also supposed to be in line with the right shoulder. The

PHOTOGRAPH 5. Correct

PHOTOGRAPH 6. Incorrect

right arm is also attached to the right side of the body. A common error made by young conductors, however, is to position the beat frame directly across the center of the body as in Photograph 7. This would make sense only if the right arm were attached to the center of the upper chest, which of course it is not.

PHOTOGRAPH 7.

Later, when using a baton, the beat frame will be fairly centered across the body. When held correctly, the baton naturally points slightly to the left placing the tip of a 12-14 inch baton across body center. For now, however, the vertical center of the beat frame should be in line with the right shoulder.

To achieve and maintain proper position of the beat frame, check yourself daily on the following: (1) that the right forearm is almost parallel to the floor when in ready position, which will keep the bottom of the beat frame in the vicinity of the solar plexis; (2) that the right hand is in line with the right shoulder, which will position the beat frame somewhat to the right of the body; and (3) that the right elbow is sufficiently raised causing the palm of the right hand to face down. Also be sure that the right arm is extended slightly forward of the body.

Of all of these, correct elbow position is the most important and also the one most often incorrect. In order for the arm to operate at peak efficiency, the upper arm must be sufficiently away from the rib cage in order for the shoulder joint to function freely. Unlike the wrist and elbow joints which operate like hinges, the shoulder joint is of the ball and socket type. When the upper arm is held too close to the body, this greatly restricts the range of motion available to the arm as a whole. As an extreme example of this restriction, squeeze both of your elbows tightly against your sides and try to conduct a fortissimo four pattern. It isn't easy, is it?

Primary and Secondary Metric Accents

To understand why beat patterns are shaped as they are, let us review the concept of primary and secondary metric accents. In four-beat meters, for example, beats one and three are primary, two and four are secondary. This means that one and three are heavy beats; two and four are lighter beats. (Some people use the terms strong and weak beats instead.) String bowing is directly related to this concept in that, in a four-beat measure, beats one and three are usually taken down bow (heavy stroke) while beats two and four are taken up bow (lighter stroke). To the conductor this means that beats one and three will be larger and beats two and four will be smaller. In the two pattern, one is large and two is smaller. In the three pattern, beat one is largest, beat two is smaller, and beat three is the smallest.

Also important in conducting is the fact that emphasis on the primary (heavy) beats is achieved through strength or weight of the gesture as well as larger beat size. Consequently the secondary (lighter) beats receive correspondingly less weight as well as being smaller in size.

Admittedly the above is a very abstract, textbook kind of approach to the subject which applies to real music only in a very general sort of way. Yet it is a concept fundamental to most traditional Western music and directly related to the way that we conduct. Our beat patterns are based on it as will be shown in the following discussion.

22

The Four Pattern

Conducting is a very subjective topic which can easily and quickly spawn arguments among both conductors and teachers. Nowhere is this more evident than in regard to beating time in four. Some believe that the ictus for all four beats should appear in the same place as in Diagram 5a. Others advocate having each ictus appear at a progressively higher level as in Diagram 5b. Diagram 5c is similar to 5b except the third beat is not as high. Diagram 5d has all beats positioned on the same horizontal plane, except for beat four which is slightly higher than the others. Still other styles of time beating exist, including the so-called delayed beat approach, but these will not be discussed here. The four styles covered

DIAGRAM 5

a.

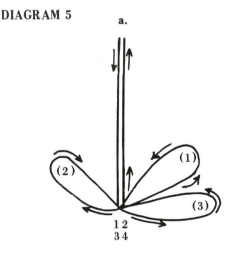

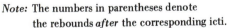

b.

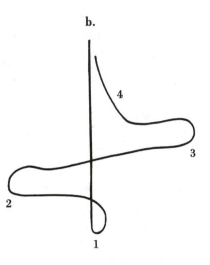

Note: The numbers in parentheses denote the rebounds *after* the corresponding icti.

c.

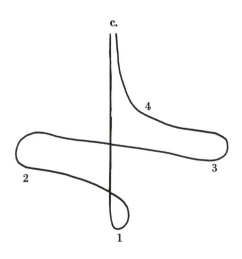

d.

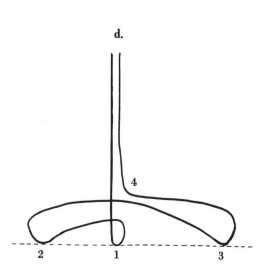

here were selected because they appear to be the ones most widely used today.

Of the four styles we prefer those shown in Diagram 5c and d. Occasionally we find Diagram 5b useful as a remedial technique for conductors whose third beat "scoops up" and is otherwise too large. We do not personally recommend the pattern in Diagram 5a. The main problem with it is that the pattern is unclear due to excessive vertical movement. All of the icti appear in the same place, thus it is not really a pattern at all. The excessive rebound necessary in order to put each ictus in the same place makes the pattern even more unclear and difficult to diagram. At the same time we know several excellent conductors and conducting teachers who use this style and teach it. You should use the style recommended by your instructor.

In Diagram 5c note that beats one and three are the largest in size (cover the largest distance) and beats two and four are smaller (cover relatively less distance). This is in direct correlation with the primary and secondary metric accents discussed earlier: The larger the beat size, the heavier the metric accent; the smaller the beat size, the lighter the metric accent.

The four pattern is used in $\frac{4}{4}$, $\frac{4}{2}$, and fast $\frac{12}{8}$ meters. It is also used in various asymmetrical meters that contain four basic beats per measure, which will be discussed in Chapter 4.

We want all readers to understand very clearly that all of the beat pattern diagrams shown in this subsection (and those in the following subsections) are to be viewed as general guidelines—approximations of what the beat patterns look like when we conduct. Numerous physical as well as musical variables associated with a given piece of music will require that alterations in the pattern be made. But one must start somewhere, and we have found the patterns shown here to be practical and functional in the teaching of young conductors.

The Three Pattern

That there are various schools of thought on how to execute the four pattern applies equally to the three pattern. Some prefer having all three beats appear in the same place, as in Diagram 6a. Others prefer each beat rising to a progressively higher level as in Diagram 6b. We happen to favor the pattern shown in Diagram 6c.

The comments made about the four styles of four pattern shown in Diagram 5 apply equally to the styles of three pattern shown in Diagram 6.

We recommend the pattern in Diagram 6c because of the lighter beat three. Also note that in accordance with the metric accent idea, beat one is the largest (thus heaviest). Beat two is smaller (lighter), and beat three is the smallest (lightest).

The three pattern is used in $\frac{3}{4}$, $\frac{3}{2}$, slow $\frac{3}{8}$, and fast $\frac{9}{8}$ meters. It is also frequently used in asymmetrical meters that contain three basic beats per measure.

24 **DIAGRAM 6**

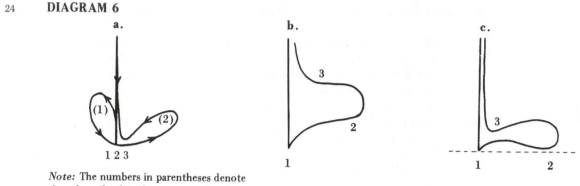

Note: The numbers in parentheses denote the rebounds after the corresponding icti.

The Two Pattern

There are four styles of two pattern available to the conductor. The differences have to do mainly with the weight and style of beat two. The four styles are grouped into two pairs for the purposes of this discussion.

The Light Beat Two style shown in Diagram 7a is the one used most often. For this reason, it should be practiced first. It is designed for musical styles and tempi that emphasize a strong beat one (primary metric accent) and a light beat two (secondary metric accent). Consequently it is the predominant type of two pattern used for marches and faster dance music.

In the Passive Beat Two style shown in Diagram 7b, the ictus for beat one is strong while the ictus for beat two is practically nonexistent. Beat two is executed as if it were a very light preparatory beat.

The Passive Beat Two style is used in those measures where the second beat is passive (musically inactive). A specific example of where both the passive and active beat two styles are used is given in Example 3. The Legato Style pattern shown in Diagram 8a is used in legato $\frac{2}{4}$ and $\frac{6}{8}$ meters. Care must be taken that the second beat is not "curled" upward too far. This constitutes excessive rebound. Keep the pattern small and clear. The Marcato Style pattern shown in Diagram 8b has a beat two which is equal in weight to beat one. It is also appropriately used for a series of two or more accents.

DIAGRAM 7

Light beat two

Passive beat two

EXAMPLE 3. Gustav Holst, Second Suite in F for Military Band, opening measures

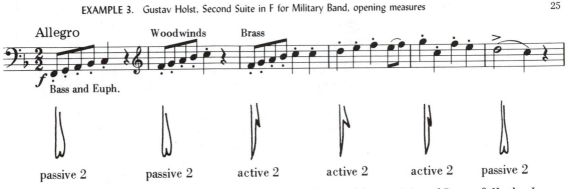

The Legato Style pattern (Diagram 8a) is called for later in the same work by Holst just cited (see Example 4). Still later in the same movement the tempo slows down and the same phrase is conducted marcato as in Diagram 8b.

DIAGRAM 8

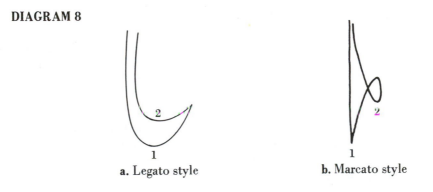

a. Legato style   **b.** Marcato style

EXAMPLE 4. Gustave Holst, Second Suite in F for Military Band, first movement, measures 47–55

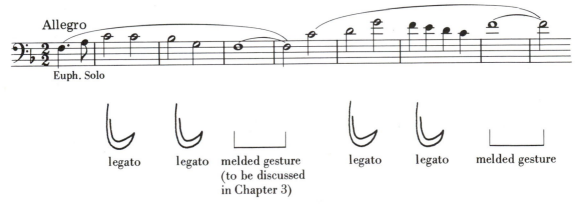

When the Legato Style pattern is erroneously used in marches and other typically nonlegato music, the following problems usually result:

1. The beat pattern becomes very unclear due to excessive rebounding. Both beats begin to look like downbeats as shown in Diagram 9a. Both beats are also equally heavy which violates the primary-secondary metric accent concept.

2. In loud dynamics in particular, the problem shown in Diagram 9b tends to predominate. The downbeat is very imprecise and unclear. The down-beat should always be straight down, not at an angle.

3. The biggest problems, however, are in the areas of tempo and style. Because of the large size and heaviness of the above patterns, the ensemble naturally responds with loud, heavy playing accompanied by a tempo which drags incessantly. The novice conductor typically reacts to this by making the beat larger and heavier in an effort to gain control. The response of the ensemble, however, is to play still more loudly and heavily, thus more slowly. The immediate solution is to use a small, light beat. The ultimate solution is to discard the Legato Style pattern in favor of the Light Beat Two pattern. Not only is the latter pattern more appropriate musically, it is also far less exhausting physically.

One final comment. . . . Experience has shown that the Light Beat Two pattern is most easily executed when the right elbow is up in its proper position. If the elbow is too low, the Light Beat Two pattern no longer feels natural; the Legato pattern feels more comfortable. Also a very low elbow usually results in the pattern shown in 9b. Therefore, to maintain good elbow height, check to see if the palm of the right hand faces downward. If not, lift the right elbow until it does.

The two pattern is designed for $\frac{2}{4}$, $\frac{2}{2}$, and fast $\frac{6}{8}$ meters. It is also used for asymmetrical meters requiring two basic beats per measure.

The One Pattern

The one pattern is conducted like a series of downbeats except that the rebound is all the way up to the top of the pattern as shown in Diagram 10a. What is essentially a straight up and down movement as shown in Diagram 10a is definitely preferred over the oval shape in Diagram 10b.

DIAGRAM 9

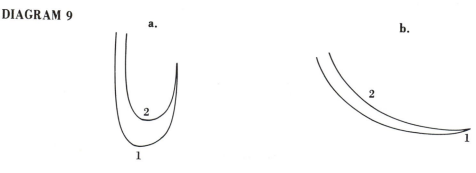

DIAGRAM 10

a.

b.

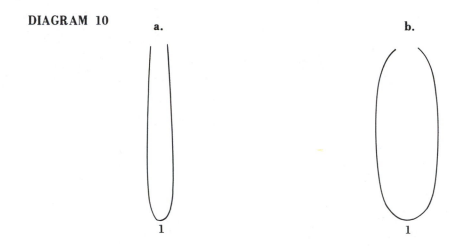

1   1

The one pattern is used mainly in very fast $\frac{2}{4}$, $\frac{3}{4}$, $\frac{2}{8}$, and $\frac{3}{8}$ meters. Occasionally it is employed in fast $\frac{4}{8}$ and $\frac{5}{8}$ meters.

Due to the small horizontal size of the one pattern and its repetitious nature, it limits the conductor's ability to indicate a crescendo or diminuendo with the right hand. To circumvent this problem in a four measure crescendo, for example, conduct these measures using a four pattern. The four pattern easily lends itself visually to a gradual increase in beat size. The same can be done in reverse, of course, for a four measure diminuendo.

Common Time-Beating Problems and Their Solutions

A good beat pattern should be clear and precise in every respect. This means that each beat should be clearly distinguished from all of the others; no two icti should be in the same place. Also, there should be no extraneous movements of the arms or body which detract from the clarity of the pattern itself.

Common time-beating problems of young conductors which violate the above criteria include excessive rebounding, "curling" or "scooping" on beat three, and a final beat in the measure which is too large. The most frequent problem of these is the first, excessive rebounding, as shown in Diagram 11, where the hand *and arm* flip upward excessively after each ictus. This makes each beat look the same, especially for ensemble performers positioned along the extreme right and left sides of the conductor. The concept of a clear beat pattern is lost; the conductor might just as well conduct a continuous series of downbeats.

The major causes of excessive rebounding are: (1) a conducting arm which is too relaxed, and (2) lack of attention to correct placement of the beats. The wrist should be flexible but not floppy. The elbow and shoulder also need to be flexible but with firm control of the surrounding musculature. Finally, the conductor needs to think horizontally in order to create sufficient distance between each ictus. With some students it has proved

DIAGRAM 11

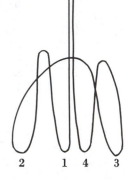

2   1 4   3

helpful to prescribe the pattern shown in Diagram 12 as a remedial technique. Practicing this time-beating style makes the conductor very conscious of beat placement. Executing the various height levels also makes excessive rebounding more difficult to do.

Another prime cause of excessive rebounding is a low right elbow. This position restricts fluid horizontal movement while at the same time promoting excessive vertical movement. Lift the elbow and immediately you will sense a freedom of movement horizontally that does not exist otherwise. Elbow height directly affects many aspects of conducting technique.

Another frequent time beating problem is that of "scooping" or "curling" of beat three as shown in Diagram 13a. This usually is also accompanied by the fourth beat being too large and too heavy. Again the primary source of the problem is insufficient control of conducting arm musculature and just plain carelessness regarding proper beat placement. The conductor needs to be sure to "place" the ictus in its

DIAGRAM 12

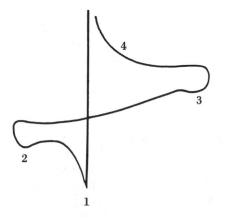

DIAGRAM 13

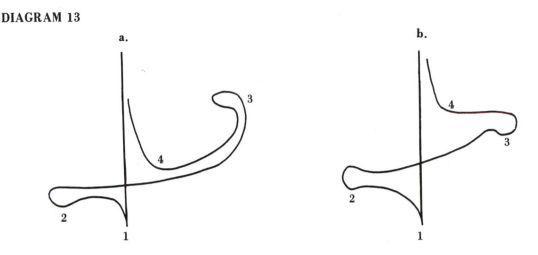

a.

b.

proper spot on the right with a downward snap of the wrist followed by a small rebound as shown in Diagram 13b. Too often the conductor merely "swings into" the third beat with no conscious effort given to conducting a clean, clear ictus. Again, practice of the pattern shown in Diagram 13b can, as a remedial technique, help the conductor learn to place the beat correctly without curling upward.

The curling-scooping problem also manifests itself in the three-beat pattern shown in Diagram 14a. The solutions for solving this problem are the same as those recommended above.

RELATED PRACTICE PROCEDURES

Each practice period should begin with a careful review of proper stance, ready position, good eye contact, and the preparatory-downbeat-cutoff sequence, which form the foundation to good conducting tech-

DIAGRAM 14

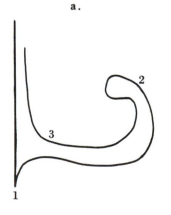

a.

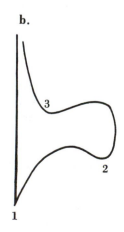

b.

30 nique. After completion of the same, practice the four-, three-, two-, and one-beat patterns next.

In the case of beat patterns, the important need for *slow* practice cannot be overemphasized. We mean very, very slow practice at first with total emphasis on accuracy and clarity. Practice the four, three, two and one patterns separately at first. Mix them as soon as you feel comfortable in doing so.

During practice check yourself repeatedly on the following points:

1. Is my right hand in line with my right shoulder?
2. Are my beat patterns clear? (Check for excessive rebounds and good horizontal movement.)
3. Am I placing the ictus of beat three correctly in the four pattern, or am I swinging into the third beat creating a curl? (The same applies to beat two of the three pattern.)
4. Is my elbow up and the palm down?
5. Are my icti clear and precise?

Remember that approximately 50 percent of your practice should be done with the eyes closed in order to focus better on kinesthetic sensations. Eventually everything you do with the hands must become second nature. This is so that you can concentrate on musical expression and identify ensemble performance errors in rehearsal. Only through development of proper kinesthetic habits will it be possible to accomplish all of these tasks simultaneously. Keep in mind that kinesthetic sensations are most easily monitored by the brain in the early stages when the movements themselves are very slow.

For maximum return in learning for the time and effort invested, we strongly recommend several brief practice sessions each day as opposed to one or two long ones. The main reason for this is that conducting technique ultimately depends on kinesthetic habit formation, not intellectual concentration. Kinesthetic habits are also best acquired through short but frequent periods of reinforcement. Therefore, the ideal is to practice manual technique six to eight or more times per day if possible. Two or three minutes between classes, five minutes before lunch, ten minutes before you go to sleep at night . . . these are good practice times—utilize them.

Another excellent practice approach is what we call "partner practice" involving two conducting students working together. While one conducts, the other observes and makes corrections. In some respects this approach is the best of all in that it forces each student, in the role of a teacher, to know and understand the skills involved in minute detail.

Other Basic Right Hand Functions

In addition to meter (pattern of the beat), the right hand should also convey the following information:

1. Tempo (speed of the beat)
2. Dynamics (size of the beat)
3. Musical style (shape and weight of the beat)

This section will be devoted to a discussion of each of these functions.

Tempo

The conductor's first responsibility is to establish the correct tempo. Correct tempo is critical to the total effect of any given piece. Simply stated, if the tempo is wrong, there is no way the music can sound right.

In compositions where a metronome marking is provided, the conductor's task in developing a "feel" for the correct tempo is greatly simplified. When no metronome marking exists, the only real clues are the generalized tempo marking (allegro, andante, lento, etc.), the conductor's general knowledge of the composer's music and musical style, plus the notational contents of the specific work under consideration.

Another important consideration is whether a given piece should be conducted in four or in two; or should a given piece in $\frac{3}{4}$ meter be conducted in three or one? The form or the type of piece often provides clear direction in this regard. For example, a Viennese waltz or Beethoven scherzo is usually in one while a Mozart minuet is normally in three. This topic will be covered in more detail in Chapter 6. For the moment suffice it to say that the decision concerning the number of beats to conduct in each measure is not to be taken lightly. An incorrect decision will result in a performance lacking in proper musical drive and intensity.

As specific exercises aimed toward developing a sense of tempo, we recommend the following:

1. With a metronome, practice the four, three and two patterns at ♩ = 60. Do the patterns separately at first; then try changing from one pattern to another without stopping in between.
2. Next practice the above patterns at ♩ = 120. Do them separately and mixed as before.
3. Do both of the above daily and gradually begin to practice tempi on both sides of 60 and 120 beats per minute.

The reason for choosing ♩ = 60 to start with is because it is easy to determine this tempo even without a metronome by simply checking the second hand on one's wrist watch. Many of us also learned to identify seconds by saying "one-thou-sand, two-thou-sand, three-thou-sand," etc., in triplets. If we double the tempo of ♩ = 60, we have 120, of course.

Dynamics

The prescription for indicating dynamic levels is really quite simple: The louder the dynamic, the larger the beat pattern; the softer the dynamic, the smaller the beat pattern. Also, extending the right arm increasingly forward as the dynamic level increases helps reinforce the increasing size of the beat pattern. Correspondingly, bringing the arm back toward the body helps indicate a reduction in dynamic level.

The above seems easy enough, but we need to be aware of the following problems (caused by natural human tendencies) connected with conducting and performance of dynamics:

1. As the dynamic gets louder, the tempo tends to get slower.
2. As the dynamic gets softer, the tendency is to go faster.

These tendencies seem to hold true for instrumentalists in particular. With singers, just the opposite often happens: faster gets louder and softer gets slower. We think it may be because of the use of words in singing but we are not sure. To solve these problems as a conductor, simply practice doing crescendi and decrescendi with a metronome. Begin at $\downarrow = 60$ or even slower and work on increasing and decreasing the size of your four and three patterns gradually. At first do one measure of crescendo followed by one measure of decrescendo. Then increase each one to two measures. Keep in mind that *each beat* must change in size, not just the first half or the second half of the measure.

Musical Style

There are three basic musical styles that the conductor must be prepared to indicate: legato, marcato, and staccato. Each style is discussed separately below.

LEGATO. Legato style is very smooth, intense, flowing, and connected. Correspondingly, the beat pattern should be designed to emphasize this by lengthening the horizontal parts of the beat pattern and decreasing the vertical aspects. To achieve these changes, the wrist must be relaxed with the palm of the hand down to allow for proper up and down movement of this pivot point. The right elbow must also be sufficiently raised to allow for free movement of the elbow and shoulder joints.

In legato at a loud dynamic, up and down movement of the wrist to define the ictus will be fairly large. In the softest, most delicate legato, the ictus must also be clearly visible via wrist movement even though the movement will be relatively small and correspondingly delicate.

In an effort to create a very soft, delicate legato, some conductors move so smoothly through their beat patterns that the icti are virtually non-existent. Such an approach should be avoided. A clear, perceptible ictus needs to be evident even in the most delicate legato in order to insure good, secure attacks as well as achieve a smooth legato style.

The ictus is the most basic element in conducting. It is the primary source of information needed by ensemble performers in order to stay together. Conductors who fail to provide consistent, clear icti usually have ensembles lacking in good rhythmic precision. Clear icti, therefore, are absolutely essential to good conducting technique.

We hasten to point out, however, that clear icti alone will not insure superior ensemble precision. Ensemble performers must also be taught to listen to each other as well as watch the conductor in order to stay together. Performers who only watch the conductor and fail to listen will have problems in ensemble intonation, balance, and blend, as well as rhythmic precision.

Probably the most common legato problem for conductors is a stiff wrist. A stiff wrist often causes the elbow joint to stiffen also. With movement only in the shoulder joint, the conductor's arm will appear immobilized as if in a plaster cast. To relax the wrist, first think of "bouncing a ball" on each beat. Often this helps relax the entire arm. If it doesn't, drop the arm at your side and shake it rag doll style. Then try again, this time exaggerating the up and down movement of the wrist while beating time very slowly. This kind of practice helps activate kinesthetic awareness to relaxed wrist motion. Maintaining a relaxed wrist in legato is absolutely essential.

There is a rather heavy, intense type of legato gesture commonly referred to as a "weighted" or "tenuto" gesture. It is used for conducting a very intense and sustained type of legato music. It involves controlled tension of the arm which appears to be pulling a heavy weight through the space between each ictus. It has been compared to "conducting with a ping pong paddle under water." This gesture will be discussed in detail in Chapter 4.

MARCATO.   In simplest terms *marcato* denotes a separated, accented style that is usually performed at louder dynamic levels. The wrist is raised slightly, snapped downward rather heavily for the ictus, and stopped briefly afterward to indicate separation before moving to the next beat. As a rule the entire arm is used fully extended in this style, especially in fortissimo. Special care should be taken to avoid excessive rebounding in marcato style, however. Keep the beat pattern as horizontal as possible in order to help maintain minimal rebounding.

STACCATO.   In simplest terms *staccato* means "short and light." In conducting, the shortness is indicated by stopping wrist movement immediately after the ictus in the form of a rapid flick of the wrist. Lightness is achieved through use of a small beat size. Thus, in a good staccato beat pattern what is seen mainly is active wrist movement, some movement of the forearm, and very little involvement of the upper arm. If the upper arm becomes active, the style moves quickly toward marcato and away from staccato.

The tendency in staccato, as in other soft dynamics, is to increase the tempo. To counteract this, practice staccato passages with a metronome.

Ultimately the best way to understand and recognize the differences among legato, marcato, and staccato conducting gestures is to observe

34   **DIAGRAM 15**

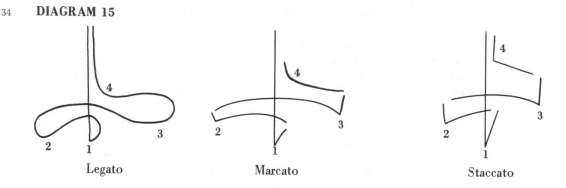

Legato   Marcato   Staccato

your instructor and then imitate each gesture immediately afterward. As a first step toward understanding, however, a diagram illustrating each of the three styles is provided (see Diagram 15). The open spaces after each ictus in the marcato and staccato styles represent a complete stop in hand movement.

Note in particular the differences between the marcato and staccato diagrams. The marcato diagram is larger, thus the dynamic level is to be louder. In addition, its rebound and the stop (open space) after each ictus is also smaller and shorter than in staccato.

USING THE BATON

To use or not to use a baton—that is the question among many musicians. While it is true that most conductors of instrumental groups use a baton and choral conductors often do not, this does not mean that use of a baton is generally not recommended in choral conducting. To the contrary we believe all students of conducting should learn to use a baton.

In this section we will discuss the purpose and function of a baton, how to select a baton and hold it properly, and how to place the ictus correctly; there is also a short discourse at the end on finger and wrist tension problems.

The Purpose and Function of a Baton

What purpose and function does a baton serve? First of all, it serves as an extension of the conductor's right hand. (We specifically say right hand rather than right arm because the pivot point for the hand and the baton is the wrist, not the elbow or the shoulder.) As an extension of the conductor's right hand, it amplifies the size of the beat pattern which makes it easier for the performers to see, especially in the back rows of larger ensembles. In the performance of works requiring large numbers of musicians, such as Beethoven's Ninth Symphony, conductors almost always use a baton. Not only does this make it easier for the performers to see the beat pattern, it also makes it physically easier for the conductor since there is less need for use of the entire arm in conducting large, expansive beat patterns.

Another important function of the baton is to make the icti more clear, especially in slower, softer passages. Here again the purpose and function of the baton is to provide greater clarity for the performers, which is probably the reason why many ensemble performers, given a choice, prefer working with conductors who use a baton.

Selecting a Baton

There is a wide variety of batons available for purchase both in terms of length and the size of the bulb held in the hand. No single baton will suit everyone; individual hand and finger sizes are as different as body heights and shapes. On the other hand, moderation should be the general rule in selecting a baton, as it should be in many other aspects of our existence. Extremely long batons and large bulbs in particular should be avoided.

We recommend use of a relatively light-weight baton, approximately twelve inches long that is well-balanced and has a medium to small bulb on the hand-held end. A well-balanced baton is one that, when held horizontally, is neither top heavy nor bottom heavy. Actually it should feel almost weightless when held in the proper position for conducting. A baton which feels heavy or imbalanced will be likely to create excessive tension in the fingers. Too large a bulb on the baton also promotes gripping by the fingers, and thus excessive tension. In both cases excessive tension in the fingers usually radiates to the wrist causing even greater problems.

Holding the Baton

There are two ways to hold a baton: one is like a snare drum stick with the baton inside the bend of the first joint of the first finger; the other is with the index finger on top of the baton and the thumb opposite the middle finger. (See Photographs 8 and 9. Note the bent thumb in both cases.)

The baton hold shown in Photograph 8 is the one we normally recommend because it is the one which feels most natural to most conducting students. If this hold does not seem comfortable, try the baton hold shown in Photograph 9 to see if it suits you better. Note in this case that the thumb is opposite the first joint of the middle finger and the index finger is extended forward.

The bulb of the baton should touch the *center* of the palm of the hand, regardless of which baton hold is used. This allows the baton to extend forward in a straight line from the elbow past the wrist while pointing slightly inward. If the baton points upward, the bulb is positioned too low in the palm. If the baton points downward, the baton bulb is above the center of the palm.

Special care should be taken that the little finger of the right hand

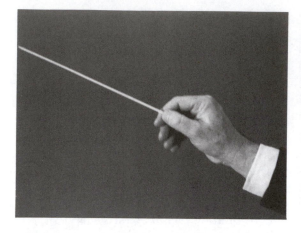

PHOTOGRAPH 8.   PHOTOGRAPH 9.

does not stick out "teacup style." When it does, this usually indicates excessive tension in the thumb, first, and second fingers. Avoid gripping the baton. As for the third and fourth fingers, let them relax downward in a natural, curved position, but without touching the baton or helping hold it in any way.

In slow legato passages, the second, third, and fourth fingers should be lifted at the knuckles and held out straighter. The fingers should look as if they were floating on air, which is essentially the same hand position you used when conducting without a baton. In marcato, the fingers should drop back down, even to the point of touching or holding the baton in extreme loud and heavy marcato music. To some, this shift in finger position may seem like a minor point, but the visual effect can be quite dramatic and amazingly effective when used properly.

Placement of the Ictus

Until now, the right hand second finger has served as the point of the beat or ictus. When using a baton, the ictus should appear in the baton tip. An aid toward making this happen is to imagine drops of dew forming on the baton tip and flicking them off each time you conduct a new ictus.

Since the baton functions as an extension of the hand, the wrist serves as the pivot point for both the baton and the hand. Therefore, the baton should not be held loosely by the thumb and index finger and allowed to flip up and down (pivot) at this point;* the wrist is the correct pivot point. But in order for the wrist to fulfill its pivot function properly, it must move up and down freely; it must not be locked or stiff. A free

---

*This incorrect position also promotes the "teacup" little finger problem discussed in the preceding section.

wrist allows the icti to appear in the tip of the baton where they should be. A stiff wrist causes the icti to appear in the heel of the hand. When this happens, the baton becomes a useless appendage which now hinders rather than helps the performers.

Finger and Wrist Tension Problems and Solutions

A major reason why some conductors do not like to use a baton is that they feel uncomfortable with it; some even say that it gets in their way. This can happen very easily, of course, and is precisely the reason why we asked that you not use a baton until now.

Another major problem that many conductors experience when first using a baton is excessive tension in the fingers which then radiates to the wrist. Two main things that contribute to this are: (1) gripping the baton tightly, especially with the second, third, and fourth fingers; and (2) using a very long, heavy baton—which may also be imbalanced—thus promoting a rather strong grip in order to hold and control the baton.

To begin solving the above problem, first change to a lighter weight well-balanced baton approximately twelve inches long. Next, concentrate on the idea of baton *hold* as opposed to baton *grip*. Baton hold means using just enough muscle energy to hold the baton securely and no more. Gripping the baton means using too many muscles, resulting in excessive tension in the fingers which radiates to the wrist and eventually to the rest of the arm. At its worst, the entire arm may begin to move stiffly as if in a plaster cast.

If these adjustments do not solve the problem, then practice beating time very slowly at first without a baton. Concentrate on relaxing the fingers and wrist. If needed, stop beating time and shake your hands and arms in rag doll fashion at your sides; then try beating time again. Once this feels comfortable, grasp the baton at about its midpoint with the left hand and begin beating time with the right hand. After beating two or three measures, let the left hand give the baton to the right hand as it moves left for beat two. Keep the beat pattern going without interruption and concentrate on maintaining a baton hold free of excessive finger and wrist tension.

LEFT HAND TECHNIQUES

The left hand has the special function of portraying and highlighting the expressive qualities of the music. Seldom should it mirror the beat pattern of the right hand. If it only duplicates the actions of the right hand, or floats aimlessly in front of the body, its special status is negated. To preserve its special status, its use has not been introduced (beyond starting and stopping the ensemble) until now.

When used appropriately, the left hand serves as a warning to the performers that something special is about to happen. That something may be an accent, ritardando, accelerando, possibly a meter change, or an entrance cue. The left hand is also used for releasing a phrase and

38

helping start a new phrase, and for helping indicate crescendo and decrescendo. Since this last function is also the one which takes longest to master, it will be discussed first.

Indicating Crescendo and Decrescendo

To use the left hand most effectively in crescendo and decrescendo, motion in two different planes must be combined: (1) up and down, and (2) away from and toward the body. Too often conducting students seem unaware of the away from and toward the body plane of movement and use only the up and down plane. The result is an awkward gesture which can be described as a ''jerky elevator ride.''

To indicate a crescendo, begin with the left hand in a neutral position against the abdomen. Lift the arm slowly and turn the left palm up as the crescendo begins. Cup the hand as if actually holding an object in the open hand, say a grapefruit. As the hand ascends to show the increase in volume, it should also move away from the body towards the ensemble. At the climax of the crescendo the hand will be approximately at chin level and the palm will actually be angled slightly back to the conductor (see Photograph 10).

To execute the decrescendo, reverse the process *slowly*. For some reason the return to the neutral position is frequently rushed through

PHOTOGRAPH 10.

resulting in a poorly executed phrase ending. At the heart of this particular problem is the tendency to flip the palm out to the ensemble as soon as the decrescendo begins. The palm should *gradually* pivot back to its original neutral position. Thus the decrescendo actually involves three simultaneous motions: (1) the hand and arm move downward, (2) they move back toward the body, and (3) the palm rotates from facing up to facing toward the ensemble (if the passage finishes at a very soft level) or to neutral position (if the passage finishes with a release). Although this may seem quite complicated, it can be achieved by practicing the three separate motions individually. Move the arm up and down, then combine that with the away from and toward the body plane. Then practice the wrist rotation needed to turn the palm properly and, finally, combine all three.

The total crescendo/decrescendo gesture should be practiced first in isolation from the right hand beat pattern, but not without music! Either sing a familiar phrase or have one played on a piano or a recording and move the left hand and arm in an expressive phrase shaping motion. Explore the space and planes of movement without being confined by time beating function. When this is comfortable, add regular right hand time beating.

The left hand crescendo-decrescendo gestures are not too difficult to describe and most students find them fairly easy to understand, especially after seeing them demonstrated by their instructor. The hard part is learning to do them properly, especially with both hands functioning simultaneously. We know of no simple solution to this challenge in coordination, but we do know that success can be achieved through lots of slow repetitive practice over a long period of time and right now is a good time to begin. As with the other conducting basics covered earlier, we recommend short but frequent practice sessions on these gestures each day. Be persistent; positive results are sure to come eventually.

Other Common Uses of the Left Hand

Besides the crescendo-decrescendo gesture, the left hand can be effective in reinforcing accents, ritardandi and accelerandi, cuing, and releasing a phrase along with starting a new one. Each of these will be discussed briefly below.

ACCENTS.   To reinforce an accent with the left hand, simply mirror the action of the right hand beginning with the preparatory beat through the ictus of the beat which is accented. Normally the beat size leading to the accented note will be larger as compared to the surrounding notes. This is assuming a regular accent (>) where the emphasis is achieved via increased tonal loudness. If a sharp accent (∧) or even a *sfz* is indicated, the ictus will probably be heavier as well. A traditional exercise for practicing accents is given in Example 5. Be sure the left hand enters on the preparatory movement prior to the accented note itself. After the accented note is finished, the left hand should return to its normal resting place.

EXAMPLE 5. Accent exercise

$\quad \downarrow = 60$

Other more advanced exercises can be created where each new accent is not so obvious. Also try two and three accents in succession. Ultimately accents need to be practiced using real music performed by live musicians.

RITARDANDI AND ACCELERANDI. To reinforce ritardandi and accelerandi, simply mirror the beat pattern of the right hand with the left hand as follows: to create a ritard, make the beat pattern gradually larger and possibly heavier, helping to slow down the tempo; in an accelerando, make the beat pattern gradually smaller and lighter, assisting in speeding up the tempo.

Related to this topic is the problem of ensembles that frequently drag or rush the tempo. When the ensemble tempo drags, the conductor's usual tendency is to make the beat larger and heavier. Seldom does this help; it only makes the tempo drag even more. (Chances are that the conductor's beat is already too large and too heavy, this being the true cause of the problem.) Instead, make the beat pattern smaller and lighter as in an accelerando. In other words, do the exact opposite of what you are tempted to do. The reverse applies when coping with a tempo that is rushed. Instead of making the beat pattern smaller and lighter, which is the usual tendency, make it larger and heavier instead, as in a ritard.

PHRASE RELEASES. The left hand can assist the right hand in releasing a phrase and in starting a new one. To execute a phrase release, the left hand joins the right hand on the last beat of the phrase and then mirrors the release movement of the right hand.

Since the release movement is difficult to describe in words, we suggest that you rely mainly on the demonstrations of your instructor to learn it. However, it is somewhat like conducting a slight tenuto followed by a quick upward flick of the hands, as in the "up tap" in snare drumming. For example, let us say the phrase ends with a dotted half note in $\frac{4}{4}$ meter. The left hand joins the right hand on the preparatory gesture and ictus of beat three. Then both hands sustain the tone until the "and" after beat three when they both flick upward for the release. Then both hands give the ictus for beat four after which the left hand returns to its normal resting place.

CUING. Cues can be given with the right hand and the head as well as the left hand. The left hand is usually used when cues are needed for performers or sections on the conductor's left side.

In executing the preparatory gesture and downbeat for the left hand cue, think of pointing and shooting a pistol. A good exercise for practice of cues on different beats is to substitute cues for each accent in Example 5 on page 40. More detailed discussion of the use of the left hand for cuing purposes is included in Chapter 3.

Recommended Excerpts in Part II for Study and Practice

America, page 142 (legato three pattern)
Overture to *Die Meistersinger,* page 145 (marcato four pattern)
Second Suite in F, page 150 (involves all types of two patterns)
Kyrie from Mass in G, page 180 (legato three pattern)
Sanctus from Mass in G, page 188 (marcato four pattern)
Second Suite in F, page 158 (three-measure decrescendo, phrase releases)

3 *Intermediate Techniques*

This chapter begins with a classification of manual techniques according to function: active, continuation, and passive gestures. The remaining topics are extensions of techniques introduced in Chapter 1: attacks and entrances occurring after the downbeat, and cutoffs other than the outside loop.

ACTIVE, CONTINUATION, AND PASSIVE GESTURES

The purpose of this section is to systematize and organize all of the various manual gestures available according to their type of function. This will allow the reader to have a better understanding of what each gesture is supposed to accomplish.

Introduction

In Chapter 1 we defined music as sound and silence aesthetically organized in time. In conducting there are two categories of gestures which deal with the sound portion of music: (1) active gestures, that are used either to start or stop the sound, and (2) continuation gestures, intended for sustaining the sound after it is started. Passive gestures, on the other hand, are designed to maintain silence; their message is "do not sing or play until I tell you." Conductors need to make a clear distinction among these three categories in their conducting.

More specifically, an active gesture is designed to make something

happen—start the group, cut them off, or make them take a breath before
performing the first note or starting a new phrase. There should be no
hesitation or indecision surrounding the active gesture. It must have a
sense of willfulness, a clearly marked point of attack or release. Gestures
in the active category include:

1. all attacks and cutoffs
2. all icti that follow the initial attack
3. all cues
4. all preparatory beats plus breathing with the ensemble

Some conductors and teachers prefer to include all preparatory beats
in the passive category. There is some logic in this since these gestures
do not actually *produce* sound. But in spite of this, their sole and primary
function is directed exclusively toward that end. For this reason we categorize all preparatory beats as active gestures.

Some conductors and teachers view all continuation gestures as passive gestures. Actually the continuation gestures are neither totally passive
or active; they possess characteristics of both. They simply continue the
sound initiated by active gestures but without articulation, accent, or
change in dynamic level. Included in this category are:

1. the continuation of a fermata
2. the continuation of a long measured note
3. melded gestures

Passive gestures, the third and final category, are designed to let the
performers know that they should be silent. There are two of these:

1. the dead beat, used to indicate specific passages of time in silence
2. the dead beat on count one of each measure of a recitative or other
   situation where the tempo is very irregular

(In some cases passive gestures may be used to mark time in a precise
manner, but this should not be mistaken as an indication to play or sing.
Keep the beat dead and inactive, not active.)

Some of the gestures listed in the preceding discussion were covered
in Chapter 1. Others will be covered later in this chapter. However, there
are four gestures that we wish to discuss as part of this section: preparatory functions, cuing, the melded gesture, and dead beats. We believe
this is information you need to know now and use in your conducting
immediately.

Preparatory Functions

Tempo, style, and dynamic level must all be communicated to the
ensemble via the preparatory beat, not the attack ictus. If the conductor
tries to communicate these things at the point of attack, then the message

is being sent one beat late. The same holds true for all types of manual conducting communication. It is *during the preparation* (the movement leading to the point of action, the space in between the icti) that the conductor must communicate what she or he wants to have happen *on the beat*. In this context be prepared (via individual practice) to execute clear preparatory gestures in the following situations:

1. a quick change of tempo, style, or dynamic level
2. an upcoming accent or tenuto
3. an entrance cue

Item 3 will be discussed in the following subsection. (Items 1 and 2 were discussed in Chapter 1).

Cuing

There are three basic kinds of cues: (1) the left hand cue, (2) the right hand or baton cue, and (3) the head cue. The left hand cue is used for cuing performers on the conductor's left while the right hand cue is used for cuing performers on the conductor's right. The head cue is most often used in softer passages where use of either hand would be disruptive to the mood or character of the music. The head cue is also sometimes used in conjunction with the left or right hand for greater emphasis when needed.

Although not mentioned until now, the eyes are the most important factor in cuing. Cues given without good eye contact are essentially worthless. Establishing eye contact two beats before the cue itself in a slow piece should be sufficient. In a fast two-pattern, at least two measures' time may be necessary. Be careful not to establish eye contact too soon, however, since the extra waiting can create needless performer anxiety.

Cues, like attacks, must be properly prepared; otherwise they are confusing and harmful rather than helpful. In Chapter 1 we said that the left hand cue should be prepared and given like "shooting a pistol." We now wish to clarify that this is appropriate mainly for marcato style music performed at a loud dynamic level. A more gentle "invitation cue" with the left hand is recommended in legato style at a soft dynamic. In other words, left hand cues should be given so that they reflect the style and dynamic indication of the right hand.

In using the right hand cue, extend the arm forward and higher on the preparation and the cue beat as if "inviting" your performers to come in. The head cue is given by simultaneously lifting the head and eyebrows on the preparation and lowering them on the cue beat. In all instances of giving cues, the conductor's eyes should be focused on the performer or perfomers concerned.

The most obvious time to give a cue is for the entrance of a soloist. Cues for multiple performers should be given for: (1) an entrance after a long rest; (2) the first entrance of a section, if other than the beginning of the piece; and (3) tricky, unique passages including isolated notes surrounded by rests. In addition, always cue cymbal crashes. Timpani entrances should almost always be cued as well. Beyond these basic guidelines, the number and type of cues given depend mainly on the ability level of your performers.

Professional singers and instrumentalists usually need very few cues; often they have the music practically memorized from having performed it so many times before. (If the piece is new, however, more cues will obviously be needed.) In the case of school musicians, cuing is especially important because of performer inexperience and related feelings of insecurity. Therefore, anything the conductor can do, especially with the eyes, to engender performer confidence will be rewarded with more secure and precise entrances. If the conductor breathes with an open mouth during the cue preparation, this also can help greatly.

A conductor problem related to cuing is shifting the entire body to the left when mainly the left side of the ensemble is performing or shifting the entire body to the right when mainly the right side is performing. When done to extremes, the opposite side of the ensemble is obliged to look at the conductor's back and can no longer clearly see the beat. Make it a rule always to stand facing front and center with the feet apart and one foot slightly forward of the other for good body balance. If you feel a need to turn slightly to the left or right, turn the upper body only at the waist but keep the feet in place. This solves the problem of one side of the ensemble not being able to see the conductor's beat. Finally, don't bend the knees, as in crouching down for a soft dynamic. It looks bad from the audience's view. Worse yet is to bounce up and down at the knees or bob the head up and down in time to the beat. Such annoying distractions should be avoided.

The Melded Gesture

"Conduct the music, don't just beat time!" How often have we heard this directive in conducting classes! To achieve this goal, proper indications of style, dynamic shading, and other elements of expression are obviously important. Another important element is the use of *melded gestures* in appropriate places in the music.

To "meld" means to combine, blend, merge together, or unite. In conducting it means combining two or more beats into a single sustained gesture. It involves giving a clear ictus at the beginning of the note with no other icti given until the beginning of the next note. Example 6 shows a clear ictus given on beat one; the baton then travels through the normal

EXAMPLE 6.

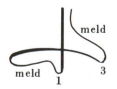

EXAMPLE 7.

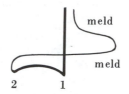

path of beat two but no ictus is given. A clear ictus is given on beat three (the start of a new note), the baton then moving through the usual path of beat four but without any ictus given.

Another instance where a melded gesture is appropriate is shown in Example 7. When the melded gesture is used as seen in this and the previous example, it can be said that we are conducting the notes (music), not the beats. To put it in another way, it means placing primary emphasis on the melodic line rather than unit beats. The function of the meld, therefore, is to sustain the sound of long tones in a phrase in a more musically productive manner.

Melded gestures are used frequently in choral conducting. Instrumental conductors also meld their gestures when appropriate. The melded gesture is most appropriate when all ensemble parts possess the same rhythm. If one is conducting the melody primarily, melded gestures can still be used, even if the other parts are rhythmically different, so long as the performers are not confused.

The Dead Beat

The *dead beat* is a passive gesture; it has no life. It is used when total silence is desired. If the dead beat shows even the slightest life at all, one or more performers may sing or play at a time when they should not.

In addition to being passive, dead beats should also be very small. This usually means use of wrist movement only, not the forearm. In contrast, a live beat preceding or following a dead beat should definitely be larger and obviously active.

Example 8 is much like the final measures of a Classical work that clearly call for use of dead beats during the rests. Use this for your first practice of dead beats.

Example 9 is typical of single rests found in music for elementary school instrumentalists. Teachers who use live beats during the rests will invariably have several players playing erroneously during the rests. If dead beats are used appropriately, it helps the players to remain silent during the rests. (It also helps meet the goal of conducting the passage properly from a musical standpoint.)

EXAMPLE 8.

EXAMPLE 9.

ATTACKS AND ENTRANCES OCCURRING AFTER THE DOWNBEAT

Three types of attacks will be discussed in this section. The first type are attacks coming on any beat of the measure other than beat one. The second are attacks starting on the offbeat (sometimes called upbeat) or other fractions of the beat. This category is called fractional beat attacks. The third category comprises fractional beat entrances—entrances of soloists or sections later on within the piece which need special attention.

Attacks on Beats Other Than Beat One

It is a basic rule in conducting that the conductor should conduct one beat (the preparatory beat) before the beat of attack (the instant that the tone is produced). This means that if the music begins on beat two, beat one is used as a preparation. If the music begins on beat three, beat two is the preparation. If the music begins on beat four, beat three is the preparation, and so forth. An illustration of this basic rule is given in Diagram 16.

Note in Diagram 16a, b, and c that the solid line always moves in a downward diagonal. This is because we believe that the first beat of any piece (no matter on what beat of the measure it falls) should have the character and, to an extent, the look (direction) of a *down*beat.

In each case there should be a very gentle ictus on the preparatory beat and a noticeably stronger ictus on the attack beat to help insure performer confidence in entering. As an additional aid, we recommend breathing during the preparatory beat with the performers. If the conductor finds it difficult to coordinate his or her breathing with the hand ges-

DIAGRAM 16

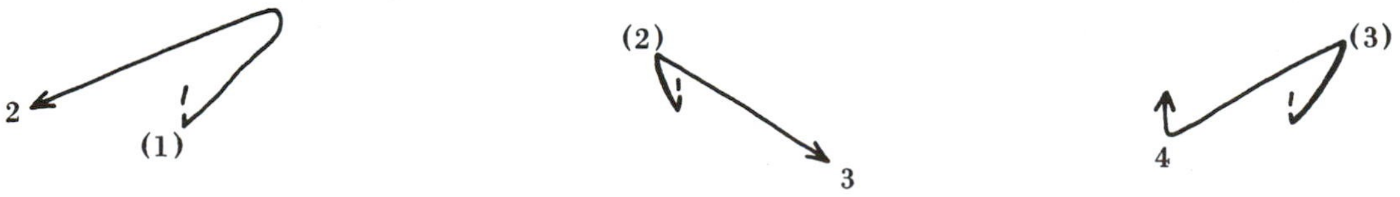

a. Attack on two   **b.** Attack on three   **c.** Attack on four

⁴⁸ DIAGRAM 17

a. Attack on two

b. Attack on three

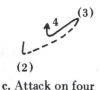

c. Attack on four

tures, then the performers will probably find it equally difficult. The conductor should slow down and make sure each movement is clear and precise.

Note that the dotted line in each instance in Diagram 16 is relatively short in length. The reason for this is to avoid giving "double preps" as shown in Diagram 17.

Note in each instance in Diagram 17 that (1) the dotted line is longer than in Diagram 16, and that (2) there is an extra movement before the beginning of the preparatory beat. This movement is usually a slight flick of the wrist implying a preparatory ictus in itself. When the hand reaches the actual preparatory ictus, several performers will invariably come in one beat too soon.

Young conductors sometimes get into the habit of giving "double preps" because they have difficulty in correctly executing the preparatory beat-attack sequences shown in Diagram 16. The problem is not the validity of the movements shown; it invariably lies with the conductor who needs additional practice time, including practice in slow motion, so that the preparatory beat-attack sequence can be executed correctly and with assurance. Remember that performers will have confidence in the conductor only if the conductor has confidence in himself. Prepare well before standing in front of an ensemble. Superior preparation is the best confidence builder that we know of. Partner practice with a conducting classmate also can be especially helpful in this particular situation.

Fractional Beat Attacks

Some compositions do not begin on the beat. They begin on an offbeat or another fraction of the beat as shown in Example 10.

EXAMPLE 10.

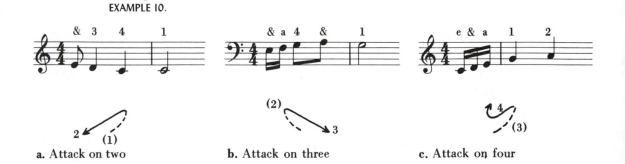

a. Attack on two   **b.** Attack on three   **c.** Attack on four

In all cases fractional beat attacks are conducted as if the attack itself were directly *on the preceding beat*. This means that the movements shown in Example 10 are exactly the same as those illustrated in Diagram 16 on page 47. Extreme care must be taken, however, that the conducting movements designated by the dotted lines in Example 10 are relatively small in size. If too large, some performers inevitably will enter one beat too soon.

Some conductors recommend that the preparatory beats shown in Example 10 should not be used. Instead the attack ictus on the beat should be the only preparation given. While we know some conductors who use this approach, we do not recommend it for the following reasons:

1. Wind players and singers do not have enough time to breathe because of the very brief preparation time, and taking a breath before the baton moves is not acceptable for the reasons cited in Chapter 1 (see p. 12).

2. There is not enough time or space to clearly indicate the exact tempo, style, and dynamics of the piece. Through repeated drill the performers will eventually learn to anticipate all of these, but at best this approach is risky, especially in faster tempi. In slow tempi it is easier to make it work satisfactorily.

Fractional Beat Entrances

Whenever a phrase begins *after* the beat the tendency of many performers is to come in late, thereby destroying the forward movement of the phrase from the onset. This problem exists in entrances such as those shown in Example 11a and b. It is even more true of an entrance like the one shown in Example 11c because of the shorter rest involved.

To counteract this problem of entering late, give a very clear preparation and a solid, firm downbeat ictus on the rest. This serves to "jolt the performers into action," thus helping get them in on time. In the case of Example 11b, a solid preparation and ictus along with increased beat size will help achieve the accent normally desired on the syncopated quarter note in addition to getting the phrase started on time.

A firm, solid preparation and ictus are recommended for all phrases and entrances beginning after the downbeat, but they are especially needed at the beginning of a work or when cuing a soloist or section. In these situations the conductor cannot afford to appear indifferent to what is going on. Worse yet, if she or he hesitates during the preparation, all is lost.

Obviously the movements called for here are difficult to describe; they are also difficult to diagram. We therefore recommend that they be

EXAMPLE 11.

a. b. c.

50   learned mainly by observing and imitating the instructor. Also refer to pages 53–57 of Green's book where she recommends using what she calls "the gesture of syncopation" to solve this problem. In this gesture, "the hand stops completely one full beat before the beat that requires the after-beat response."* Then there is a sudden, staccato-like movement to the entrance beat. The performers respond on time after the beat.

CUTOFFS OTHER THAN THE "OUTSIDE LOOP"

There are four kinds of cutoffs (also called releases) in addition to the "outside loop" introduced in Chapter 1. There is the "inside loop," rapid cutoff, single-handed cutoff, and the phrase release. Cutoffs, like attacks, are usually best done with both hands, but not always. There are times when either the right hand alone or the left hand alone is preferred.

The Loop Cutoffs

The outside and inside loop cutoffs are so named because of the direction of their movement (see Diagram 18).

The outside loop was the cutoff introduced first because it is the one used most often. Specific examples are full measure fermatas and long final notes. The inside loop is used for cutoffs *after* the last beat in the measure and sometimes after beat two in the four pattern. Actually the choice between the two depends mainly on where the hands need to be in preparation for the next entrance. Examples 12 and 13 illustrate this process.

Rapid Cutoffs

Rapid cutoffs are ones generally used on one-beat notes as shown in Example 14.

The cutoffs above are indicated via firm snaps of the wrists on beats two and four. Snapping shut the fingers of the left hand on each cutoff further aids the process.

In slower tempi, a half loop can be used to control releases more precisely as seen in the Andante version of Example 15.

In the Allegro version of Example 15 there is no time for any kind

DIAGRAM 18

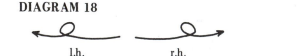

l.h.   r.h.

a. Outside loop

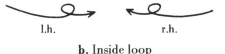

l.h.   r.h.

b. Inside loop

*Elizabeth A.H. Green, *The Modern Conductor*, 4th ed. (Englewood Cliffs, NJ: Prentice Hall, 1987) p. **53**.

EXAMPLE 12.

outside loop

EXAMPLE 13.

inside loop

EXAMPLE 14.

EXAMPLE 15.

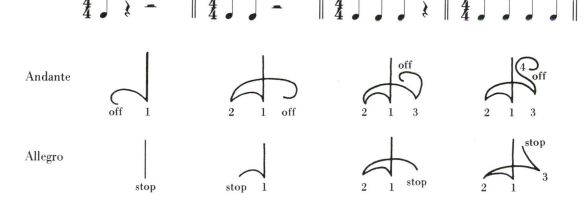

of cutoff indication, thus the solution is simply to stop the baton on the ictus of the final note in each instance. Also use both hands on the final note. After stopping all movement, freeze both arms in place. Then after a few seconds, drop the arms slowly at your sides.

If the composition, movement, or section ends on a fractional part of the beat or a division of the beat, it is conducted the same as a full unit beat (see Example 16).

EXAMPLE 16.

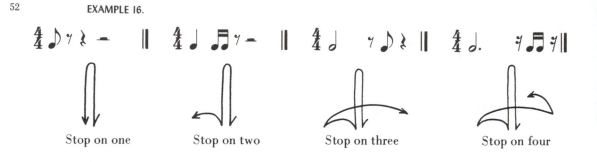

Stop on one   Stop on two   Stop on three   Stop on four

The Single-Handed Cutoff

There are times when one section needs to sustain a note while another section needs to drop out. If the section dropping out is to the conductor's left, then the left hand should execute the cutoff (usually an outside loop) while the right hand holds. If the section dropping out is on the conductor's right, then the role of each hand is reversed.

The Phrase Release

As the term implies, the phrase release is used at phrase endings to provide "breathing space" for the music and performers. The difficulty of this gesture is that the musical pulse must not stop or pause, but must continue with the next beat to the following phrase. This dual function of closing one phrase and instantaneously preparing the next sound is challenging to portray.

It can be helpful to think of the combined release/preparatory motion as having the feeling of lift or an upward motion, while the following sound-making gesture will be generally downward in direction. The phrase release should be used in those situations where ensemble releases are ragged and conductor assistance is clearly needed. Command of this gesture is vital to singers and wind players to unify inhalation rhythmically and to reinforce proper breathing technique. It is best learned through imitation of your conducting teacher.

Conducting Fermatas

There are three types of fermatas that one must learn to conduct, as shown in Example 17. These gestures can be mastered by combining some of the techniques that have already been presented.

In Example 17a the release of the fermata is the preparatory motion for the next beat. This should look and function like the phrase release cut-off. The preparatory motion must re-establish the tempo, dynamic, and style of the following phrase.

Example 17b shows the fermata followed by a cesura symbol (//). In this case the loop cutoff is used and it must come to a complete stop before the new preparatory motion is given. Note that a new preparatory

EXAMPLE 17.

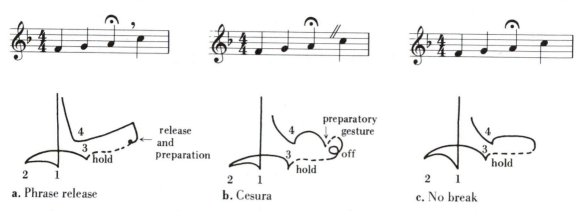

a. Phrase release   **b.** Cesura   **c.** No break

Note: Practice the three fermata types on all beats of the measure (1, 2 and 4 as well as beat 3)

gesture for beat four must also be given after the cut-off. Depending on the musical context, this pause will be somewhat longer than the break in the first example.

In Example 17c the baton does not stop at all, indicating that there should be no break in the sound after the fermata. This may be the most difficult of the fermatas because of the temptation to move the hand abruptly to start the new beat. This may then be interpreted as a release.

In our opinion the hand or baton should not stop during the "holding" of the fermata itself. To continue the sound, keep the baton moving slowly. When the baton stops, the sound stops. (The dotted line in Example 17 denotes slow movement of the baton during the fermata.) Only in Example 17b does the baton come to a complete stop to indicate the silent pause of the cesura.

As a general rule, do not conduct a cesura unless one appears in the score. At most, conduct a phrase release to end the fermata. Use your musical ear and intuition to decide if perhaps the fermata should be conducted with no break at all as in Example 17c. In choral works the text and its punctuation will help answer the question of whether to break the sound or not.

How long should the fermata be? It varies depending on the musical context. We have heard it said that a quarter note fermata should be held twice its normal value. This is a gross generalization. In the chorales of J.S. Bach, for example, the fermata symbol should be treated more like a phrase ending indicator rather than a true fermata. Traditionally these fermatas are held very little if at all with a short breath release used between phrases. Fermatas in music of other composers are treated differently.

With both the fermata and cesura, the conductor must try to determine the composer's intentions for this structural device. Is it being used

54 to close a major section of the composition, to emphasize a particular chord or word, or merely to provide a momentary pause in the musical motion? Careful score study will help provide the answers.

Recommended Excerpts in Part II for Study and Practice

America, page 142 (♩. melds in measures 6 and 14)

Chester, page 147 (numerous ♩ and ○ melds)

Overture to *The Italian Girl in Algiers*, page 152 (dead beats, *sfz* accents, soft slow staccato followed by legato)

Slavonic Dance, Op. 46, No. 1, page 155 (fermata, one pattern, accents)

Christ in the Stranger's Guise, page 164 (♪ anacrusis, fermatas, slow legato two pattern)

Scheherazade, page 170 (♫ anacrusis, slow legato two pattern)

Hail to Thee, Jesus Kind, page 176 (contains fermatas on every beat)

Kyrie from Mass in G, page 180 (numerous ♩ melds)

Beethoven, Symphony No. 5, page 194 (opening fermatas, use of one pattern)

Sinfonia, page 172 (cuing, marcato four pattern)

"How Lovely is Thy Dwelling Place," page 174 (cuing, slow legato three pattern)

Et in terra pax, page 160 (cuing, legato three pattern)

4 *Advanced Techniques*

This chapter includes entirely new material concerning asymmetric and changing meters, and divided beats. This is followed by a section on practice procedures. The chapter ends with a discussion of the importance of facial expression and communication with the eyes.

ASYMMETRIC AND CHANGING METERS

There are two variables that distinguish asymmetric meters from the more traditional simple and compound meters. First of all, some asymmetric meters contain an odd number of beats per measure (like five and seven). Secondly, in faster tempi all asymmetric meters are made up of various rhythmic groupings of unequal length. The most common rhythmic groupings used are twos and threes. Expressed in eighth note notation, a grouping of two is ♫, a grouping of three is ♫♩.

Asymmetric rhythmic groupings can be used in various combinations or permutations. In fast $\frac{5}{8}$ meter, for example, two combinations are possible: 2 + 3 and 3 + 2. In fast $\frac{7}{8}$ meter three combinations of two and three are possible, as shown in Example 18.

EXAMPLE 18.

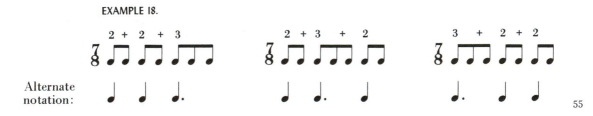

Alternate notation:

To those having limited experience with asymmetric meters, dealing with unequal rhythmic groupings in particular can be quite confusing at first, if not downright frustrating and upsetting. The beats feel top-heavy or lopsided—and they are. As a result, some performers (and sometimes conductors as well) will try to even out the beats by slowing down some groupings while speeding up others. To solve this problem let a metronome tick eighth notes (slowly at first) while counting the groupings aloud and tapping the foot on count one of each rhythmic group. Gradually increase the speed while continuing to count and tap your foot. Once the unequal foot-tap can be done easily and naturally at any reasonable speed, then one is able to internalize the unequal rhythmic groupings and beats. When this happens, you have got it!

This section is divided into four subsections. The five patterns are discussed first, followed by the seven patterns. Next, fast tempo two, three, and four patterns are covered. The section ends with a discussion of changing meters.

The Five Patterns

In slow five-beat meters two different beat patterns are needed, because two different rhythmic combinations are possible (see Diagram 19a and b below).

Note that the 3 + 2 pattern above is much like the six pattern (seen to its immediate right) except that the sixth beat is missing. The 2 + 3 pattern, on the other hand, resembles the four pattern (seen to its immediate right) except that an extra beat (beat five) has been added. Also note in Diagram 19a that the movements leading to beats one and four are the largest ones. In Diagram 19b, the movements leading to beats one and three are the largest. This is in line with the metric accent concept discussed in Chapter 1, which is another reason why the six pattern and four

DIAGRAM 19

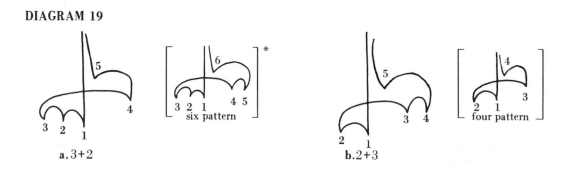

a. 3+2   b. 2+3

*The six pattern will be discussed in detail later in this chapter.

DIAGRAM 20

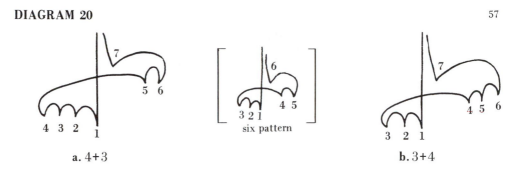

a. 4+3   six pattern   b. 3+4

pattern are used here as a basis for comparison. In both comparisons, the metric accents coincide.

The Seven Patterns

In slow seven-beat meters there are two beat patterns available for the 4 + 3 and 3 + 4 combinations that exist (see Diagram 20a and b).

Note that the 4 + 3 pattern is much like the six pattern except that an extra beat (beat four) is added in the first half of the pattern. The 3 + 4 pattern is also like the six pattern except for the added seventh beat. Note also that the size of the movements in both cases is consistent with the metric accents called for by the rhythmic groupings specified.

Actually, the 4 + 3 and 3 + 4 combinations in slow $\frac{7}{4}$ and $\frac{7}{8}$ are not used very often, probably because the notation and the beat patterns tend to be somewhat unwieldy. Basically the same musical effect is achieved via the notations shown in Example 19.

Fast Tempo Asymmetric Beat Patterns

The existence of unequal rhythmic groupings (mainly twos and threes) in fast tempo asymmetric meters automatically means that the beats themselves will also be unequal in time duration. For example, in

EXAMPLE 19.

58   **DIAGRAM 21**

a. 3+2   **b.** 2+3

fast $\frac{5}{8}$ a 2 + 3 grouping translates into an unequal two pattern based on a ♩ + ♩. time duration relationship. When there are three rhythmic groups, an unequal three pattern is required. Four rhythmic groups call for an unequal four pattern.

It is precisely these unequal or uneven beats that give asymmetric meters their unique quality. The listener's ear in effect perceives off beat syncopated-type accents occurring on the first note of each rhythmic grouping, as in ♫♪ ♪♪ ♫♪. This kind of unequal pulse gives the music a special lilt; in effect it "kinda makes it swing."

A principle that applies to all fast asymmetric meters is that the beat patterns used should duplicate their regular meter counterpart as closely as possible. For example, $\frac{5}{8}$ meter conducted in fast two should resemble the two pattern used to conduct $\frac{2}{4}$ or $\frac{2}{2}$. A three-beat rhythmic combination of 3 + 3 + 2 in fast $\frac{8}{8}$ meter should resemble the three pattern used for $\frac{3}{4}$ or $\frac{3}{2}$. Using this principle as a basis, one should be able to create a logical beat pattern for any kind of fast tempo asymmetric meter that one may encounter.

THE UNEQUAL TWO PATTERN.   The unequal two pattern is used mainly in fast $\frac{5}{8}$ or $\frac{5}{4}$ meters that contain two unequal rhythmic groupings as shown in Diagram 21a and b. Note the counting system used in both instances. This type of counting (beat counting) is recommended for all other unequal beat patterns since it is easier to feel rhythmically and easier to keep track of mentally. The metric weight of count one in each instance also helps provide the kind of unequal lilt associated with asymmetric meters.

THE UNEQUAL THREE PATTERN.   The unequal three pattern is most commonly used in fast seven- and eight-count meters like $\frac{7}{8}$ and $\frac{8}{8}$ with three rhythmic groupings as shown in Diagram 22a and b.

THE UEQUAL FOUR PATTERN.   The unequal four pattern is most commonly used in fast nine-, ten-, and eleven-count meters like $\frac{9}{8}$, $\frac{10}{8}$, and $\frac{11}{8}$ with four rhythmic groupings as shown in Diagram 23a and b.

DIAGRAM 22

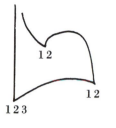

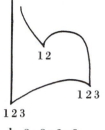

a. 3+2+2=7   **b.** 3+3+2=8

DIAGRAM 23

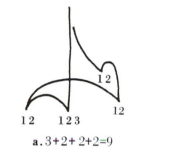

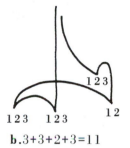

a. 3+2+2+2=9   **b.** 3+3+2+3=11

THE ASYMMETRIC ONE PATTERN.   The only time the one pattern is used in asymmetric meters is in fast $\frac{5}{8}$ with consecutive equal eighth notes. This kind of fast $\frac{5}{8}$ meter usually appears as a single measure or possibly two measures in a changing meter context as shown in Example 20.

Changing Meters

It is assumed that most readers of this text are reasonably familiar with changing meters as a result of having had direct contact with them as performers. For those whose background in this area is somewhat limited, the following basic information is provided.

EXAMPLE 20.

*Even though this measure is also conducted in one, $\frac{3}{8}$ is not considered to be an asymmetric meter as is $\frac{5}{8}$.

EXAMPLE 21.

The key to unlocking the changing meter puzzle is to determine which note value remains constant, serving as a "common denominator" from one measure to another. In Example 22, this note value is the eighth note. If there is apt to be any confusion in this regard, the composer usually specifies the note value in the score, as in measure two of Example 21. If the note value is meant to change from one measure to another, the composer will so indicate, as in measure four of Example 21a.

Mention should be made here about the use of proportional meter changes in the Renaissance period as shown in Example 21b. Note-value equivalence markings such as the one seen above the $\frac{3}{4}$ meter signature were not included by Renaissance composers. Even when equivalency markings are included by modern editors, they are not always correct. (For further information, begin with the *Harvard Dictionary of Music* article on this topic. Other information is found in the bibliography of this text, beginning on page 130.

The notation of changing meters and asymmetric rhythmic groupings by some composers is very logical and very easy to conduct; in other cases it is not. Two examples of the latter are shown in Example 22 below. In both cases we assume that the three measures fit together musically so that there is no need for separate downbeats. This allows us to combine the three measures in each case into single measures of $\frac{7}{8}$ and $\frac{9}{8}$ making the passages easier to conduct and easier to follow (see Example 22).

A reverse kind of problem exists where an asymmetric meter with obvious unequal beats is "camouflaged" within a regular simple or compound meter. Beethoven and other pre-twentieth-century composers did

EXAMPLE 22.

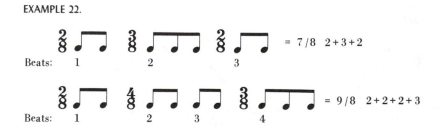

EXAMPLE 23.

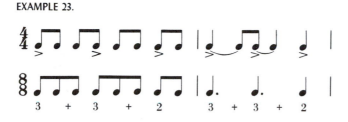

some of this during a time when asymmetric and changing meter signatures were not widely used. Much more obvious use of asymmetric camouflage is found in "school music" of the 1950s and early '60s. Example 23 illustrates one of the more frequent patterns used. Despite the $\frac{4}{4}$ time signature and related notation, we recommend using a three pattern as if it were noted in $\frac{8}{8}$ meter. The reason for this is simple: it makes much more *musical* sense to conduct it in three rather than four.

DIVIDED BEATS

When the tempo is so slow that the regular beat pattern feels awkward and looks stilted, divided beats are probably needed. The function of divided beats is to maintain a feeling of forward musical movement and to provide a clear, precise tempo. If divided beats fail to achieve this, then either they are not really needed (the regular beat pattern will suffice) or the conductor's use of divided beats is confusing. The main purpose of this section is to help you avoid the latter problem.

The term "divided beats" will be used throughout this discussion rather than the term "subdivide" which is a misnomer. Dividing the beat in simple and compound time means *dividing* the unit beat into the next smallest value: dividing the quarter note into two eighth notes and the dotted quarter into three eighth notes in compound meter (see Example 24a). Subdividing the beat means dividing the quarter and dotted quarter a second time, this time into sixteenth notes (see Example 24b). In reality, then, as conductors we *divide* the beats in very slow tempi; we do not actually *subdivide*.

Divided beats are used in simple and compound meters and in three- and four-beat asymmetric meters. Each of these topics will be treated separately in this section.

EXAMPLE 24.

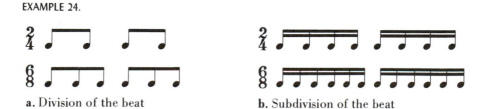

a. Division of the beat   **b.** Subdivision of the beat

DIAGRAM 24

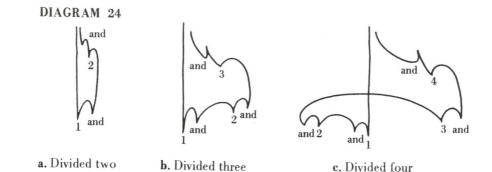

a. Divided two   **b.** Divided three   **c.** Divided four

Patterns in Simple Meters

The key factors in conducting divided beats are maintaining beat pattern clarity and making an obvious difference between strokes on the beat and those after the beat. If all are the same size, confusion results. Afterbeat pulses usually are lighter and have less rebound.

Lack of attention and carelessness make for time beating that is nothing more than an indistinguishable hodge-podge of hand movements. This kind of "flailing of the air" can easily happen in conducting regular beat patterns, of course, but when it happens in patterns employing divided beats, it is especially frustrating. The result is confusion for the conductor as well as the performers. No one knows for sure where the conductor is within the measure or, worse yet, knows where one measure ends and another begins. At the very least, the downbeat should *always* be large and clear. This will help the performers find their place if lost in the preceding measure. The other beats in the measure also need to be clear for the same reason.

Divided beat patterns in two, three, and four in simple time are illustrated in Diagram 24. Note that the basic shape of the corresponding regular two, three, and four patterns is closely maintained.

Patterns in Compound Meters

Maintaining good beat pattern clarity is especially challenging when conducting compound meters. This is due to the large number of beats conducted, especially in slow $\frac{9}{8}$ and $\frac{12}{8}$ meters as shown in Diagram 25. In fact the problem can quickly get out of control unless the patterns are practiced very slowly with full concentration on proper placement of each basic beat. Note that the divided two, three, and four patterns in Diagram 25 correspond to the basic shape of the regular two, three, and four patterns introduced in Chapter 1.

In Diagram 26 there are alternate ways to conduct slow $\frac{6}{8}$, $\frac{9}{8}$, and $\frac{12}{8}$. Some experienced conductors and instructors may be wondering why these so-called alternate patterns were not introduced first. The answer is that it is simply a matter of personal preference. We like the height and the horizontal motion of the last three beats in Diagram 25 because these unique motions issue a clear signal that beat one will immediately follow.

DIAGRAM 25

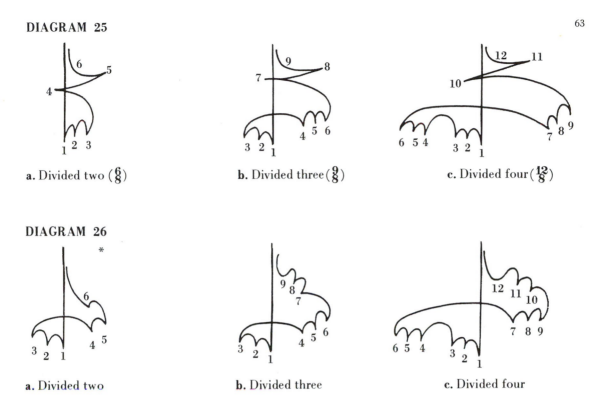

a. Divided two ($\frac{6}{8}$) **b.** Divided three ($\frac{9}{8}$) **c.** Divided four ($\frac{12}{8}$)

DIAGRAM 26

a. Divided two **b.** Divided three **c.** Divided four

*This type of pattern is sometimes referred to as the "German six" while the pattern in Diagram 25a is called the "Italian six"

And yet we have no strong feelings against the alternate patterns above. The student should follow the advice of the instructor.

That a decision has been made to divide the beats does not mean that every beat and every measure has to be divided. Notes one beat long or longer often require no division of the beat; the regular beat pattern or even a melded gesture may be in order. Use your own good judgement and the advice of your instructor in this regard. The ultimate goal is to be musical. Pedantic use of divided beats for every note in every measure defeats this goal.

The Asymmetric Divided Three

In slow $\frac{7}{4}$ or $\frac{7}{8}$ meter that consists of three rhythmic groupings, a divided three pattern should be used as shown in Diagram 27.

Note in Diagram 27a and b that the basic shape of the regular three pattern has been maintained. In Diagram 27c the third basic beat (5, 6 and 7) uses the same lateral motions as those recommended for $\frac{6}{8}$, $\frac{9}{8}$, and $\frac{12}{8}$ discussed earlier. We believe it gives a clearer signal of the approaching downbeat. We also recommend its use in all slower asymmet-

64   **DIAGRAM 27**

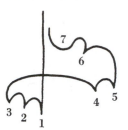

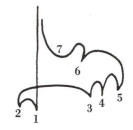

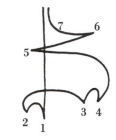

a. 3+2+2   **b.** 2+3+2   **c.** 2+2+3

DIAGRAM 28

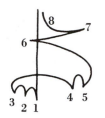

a. 3+2+3= 8 beats   **b.** 3+3+2   **c.** 2+3+3

DIAGRAM 29

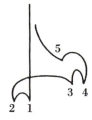

a. 2+2+1= 5 beats   **b.** 2+1+2   **c.** 1+2+2

ric meters when the last beat of the measure has a rhythmic grouping of three.

$\frac{8}{8}$ meter presents the following 3 + 2 combinations to be conducted with a divided three pattern: 3 + 3 + 2, 3 + 2 + 3, 2 + 3 + 3. In Diagram 28 only the *first* of three possible rhythmic combinations in an eight-beat meter is diagramed for you. Can you diagram the other two combinations?

Similarly in Diagram 29 only the *first* of three possible rhythmic combinations in a five-beat meter is diagramed for you. Try to diagram the other two yourself.

DIAGRAM 30

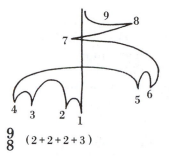

$\frac{9}{8}$ (2+2+2+3)

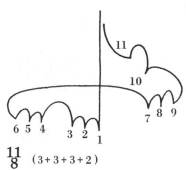

$\frac{11}{8}$ (3+3+3+2)

The Asymmetric Divided Four

The divided four pattern is normally used when the top number of the time signature is a nine, ten, or eleven in a slow tempo. The usual rhythmic groupings employed are still twos and threes. In Diagram 30, two asymmetric divided four patterns are done for you. Practice diagraming the other possible four patterns in 9, 10, and 11 on your own.

Realize that the asymmetric divided four pattern (and even the divided three pattern) are not used very often. Used much more frequently are the unequal two, three, and four patterns in faster tempi as discussed in the previous section.

PRACTICE PROCEDURES

The topics included in this section are daily warmup and practice of fundamentals, eliminating excessive tension, improving the weighted legato gesture, and principles of remedial learning.

Daily Warmup and Practice of Fundamentals

All good performing musicians use some kind of systematized warmup routine each day. Brass players, for example, rely heavily on long tones and lip slurs while other musicians concentrate on scales and arpeggios or various vocal exercises. A daily warmup routine is no less important for conductors than it is for other performers. A good warmup period is the foundation of a good practice/study session.

Knowing how to warm up properly is the first step. In this regard the animal world gives us an important clue. Surely all of us have observed a housecat on first awaking from a deep sleep. The cat begins by very slowly stretching the large body muscles. All body movements that follow, such as walking, are usually very slow and deliberate at first. Fine athletes operate in similar fashion. They know it is foolhardy to engage immediately in very fast or strenuous activities without sufficient warmup and slow practice. In the same way, the conductor should begin by slowly doing the range-of-motion exercises prescribed in Chapter 1. Then do all of the fundamentals described in the first two chapters in the order presented.

Finally, make up practice exercises based on specific problems found in the scores you are currently preparing for performance.

Two final comments: (1) always warm up and practice in front of a mirror, and (2) do your practice of manual technique without looking at any music. Concerning the latter, your visual attention should be devoted entirely to watching your movements in a mirror. The rest of your attention should focus on kinesthetic sensation of correct movements.

Eliminating Excessive Tension

Excessive tension in the shoulder is a big problem for some conductors. If the source of the tension is actually in the shoulder muscles, the range-of-motion exercises discussed in Chapter 1 may be all that is needed to solve the problem. But it is also very possible that the real source of the problem lies elsewhere, such as excessive tension in the neck area, lower back, or the large muscles of the legs. If this is true, then the following exercises may be in order. All are to be done in a standing position.

1. With your hands on your hips, gently move your head up and down five times, then move it gently from side to side five times.
2. Now gently rotate your upper body at the waist five times clockwise, five times counterclockwise.
3. Slowly do some deep knee bends and also run in place for at least one minute.
4. Between each of the above exercises, take up to five deep breaths, inhaling very slowly and exhaling very slowly.

If excessive tension manifests itself in an elbow joint that is functionally immobile, then the following exercises are recommended:

1. While the instructor or other student holds the conductor's upper arm in a stationary position, the conductor practices beating a very small four-pattern using the wrist only at first, then adding the forearm. (When practicing alone, the conductor can immobilize the upper arm by holding it against a wall while standing in a diagonal position facing away from the wall.)
2. The conductor secures the right elbow on a desk or table as if preparing to "Indian wrestle." Then conduct only with the forearm.
3. To improve horizontal movement, secure the upper arm as in Exercise 2 above and move the forearm to the left and right, back and forth. Imagine that you are moving your hand across the smooth surface of water that is perfectly still.

Not all elbow problems are due to excessive tension and stiffness. Occasionally one sees a right elbow that seems to "bounce" up and down in rhythm to the beat. Such elbow movement is distracting and unnecessary. The problem may be solved through practice of Exercises 1 and 2 above.

Improving the Weighted Legato Gesture

Some slow legato music is meant to be performed with great intensity and emotional import, a specific example being the Berceuse in Stravinsky's *Firebird* Suite beginning with the bassoon solo. Another example is the melody leading to "the big climax" of Ravel's *Daphnis and Chloe* Suite for orchestra. The term "tenuto gesture" is sometimes used to describe the type of conducting arm movement needed; however, we find that the term *weighted legato gesture* more accurately describes what is really going on.

To communicate the intensity and emotional import of slow legato music to the ensemble, the conductor's hands need to convey an image of resistance, a strong pull to each beat. To create this image of resistance and pull, think of pulling a strong, thick piece of taffy through each beat. Better yet, do some actual time beating under water in a swimming pool. If a swimming pool is not available, then fill a bathtub full of water. You can experience three degrees of resistance as follows:

1. Put your hand in the water up to your wrist and move it back and forth.
2. Put your forearm in the water up to the elbow and move it back and forth.
3. Put the entire arm in the water up to the shoulder and move it back and forth.

Another aid to developing a feeling of resistance is to clip a large paper clamp onto the tip of your baton. Be careful that this does not cause you to start gripping the baton. Experiment with different sizes of paper clamps until you find one of the proper weight for your practice needs.

Principles of Remedial Learning

Remedial learning has to do with getting rid of bad habits by replacing them with new, desired ones. It means relearning and retraining.

There are two principles of remedial learning. The first principle involves going from one extreme to another, exaggerating the process, even to the point of absurdity. The reason for going to extremes is that the mere suggestion of raising the elbow higher, for example, usually means that the student will raise it only half the needed amount. (To the student even this small amount of change feels significant.) To really experience the necessary kinesthetic sensations, however, the student should raise the elbow twice as high as the correct position (exaggerate) in the practice sessions. Then in the course of conducting a piece later when his or her concentration is focused on the music, the elbow will usually drop down to the correct height.

As another example of the above principle, let us say that the student's gestures look tense and awkward. To solve this, slow the tempo way down and make the gestures much larger. Exaggerate the movements. Then decrease the size of the gestures and increase the speed gradually while maintaining movements that are relaxed and under control.

The second remedial learning principle involves changing the immediate performance conditions, i.e., changing to a different size or type of baton, or using a paper clamp on the baton tip. For example, let us say that the conductor is gripping the baton excessively, causing a stiff wrist. The bulb may be too large or the baton may be too big, long, and heavy in general. Changing to a smaller baton often helps immediately. If not, the solution may be to stop using a baton entirely for one week or longer. Then add the use of a small, light-weight baton.

Having provided these two remedial learning principles, we hope that the readers will find many ways to apply them on their own in solving problems in teaching and learning.

THE NONMANUAL ASPECTS OF CONDUCTING

Like the actor, the conductor must learn to communicate with facial expressions and through eye contact. Such communication is as important to good conducting as is clear and precise manual technique. These two topics comprise the content of the final section of this chapter.

Facial Expression

There can be no doubt that facial expression has a direct impact on a conductor's overall effectiveness (or lack of it). The conductor with a cold, expressionless "stone face" can never be successful no matter how good his or her manual technique may be. Judicious use of appropriate facial expression, therefore, is an integral part of the conducting art, especially from the standpoint of musical expression.

Appropriate facial expression is not something one contrives by standing in front of a mirror and moving facial muscles until the face "looks just right." Like a good actor the conductor must learn to live and feel the part, to become so absorbed in the role as to "lose" himself or herself. The first step in this direction is achieved by really knowing one's score. This usually causes some appropriate facial expression to occur naturally. But in order to be fully effective, every conductor needs to practice "acting out" the musical mood he or she wishes to convey to the ensemble. In choral music this task is somewhat simplified by the existence of a text. The words can be a specific guide to mood, emotion, and the musical content to be portrayed by the conductor. When words are not available, other approaches can be used as described below.

One way is to use one's imagination to create mental pictures of the mood desired. Better yet is to recreate a mental picture based upon one's own past experiences. If the musical mood is joyful and triumphant, think of the most joyful and triumphant experiences in your life. If the mood is somber, try to recall how it felt to experience a very somber occasion, such as a funeral perhaps. Put yourself in the picture; try to feel the part.

Communicating with the Eyes

To conduct is to communicate. At the most basic level conductors communicate with hand gestures. At a more artistic, musical level they also communicate via facial expression and particularly the eyes. This point was made especially clear to one of the authors during an interview of Leopold Stokowski on the CBS television show, *Sixty Minutes,* the week before he died. The interviewer at one point made reference to hand gestures as *the* mode of communication. Stokowski responded immediately and rather brusquely by pointing to his own eyes and saying. "The eyes! We conduct with the eyes!" In this connection, we ask you to consider human communication on a one-to-one level. We talk using words but the way we really communicate with each other is with our eyes. When with someone who will not look us in the eye, we tend to become suspicious of that person. At the very least we become frustrated because of the lack of direct eye contact. Therefore, do not neglect the use of good eye contact in conducting. It is essential to good communication between conductor and performers.

Recommended Excerpts in Part II for Study and Practice

Tschaikowsky, Symphony No. 6, page 178 (begins on "and" after beat three, uses lots of crescendi and decrescendi)

Star-Spangled Banner, page 184 (begins on the third beat, phrase releases, fermatas)

Londonderry Air, page 167 (begins on beat two, weighted gestures, melds at ends of phrases followed by phrase release, two-measure crescendo and diminuendo)

"Nimrod" from *Enigma Variations,* Op. 36, page 192 (weighted gestures in three)

Bizet, Symphony No. 1 in C, page 197 (in slow 9, lots of crescendi and diminuendi)

Deck the Halls, page 201 (fast $\frac{7}{8}$ meter using $3+2+2$ and $2+2+3$)

"Ase's Death" from *Peer Gynt,* Op. 46, No. 2, page 204 (in four, weighted gesture, phrase releases, numerous crescendi and diminuendi)

Voyager's Song from *Three Thoughts from Thoreau,* page 208 (fast $\frac{7}{8}$ and changing meters)

Finale from *Firebird* Suite, page 209 (slow seven pattern using $3+2+2$ and $2+2+3$)

Promenade from *Pictures at an Exhibition,* page 212 (changing meters including five, six, and divided three patterns)

Glory to God in the Highest, page 215 (changing meters: $\frac{2}{4}$, $\frac{3}{8}$, $\frac{5}{8}$, and $\frac{3}{4}$)

Petroushka, page 218 (changing meters: $\frac{3}{8}$, $\frac{4}{8}$, $\frac{2}{8}$, and $\frac{5}{8}$.

5 *Beyond Manual Technique*

The main thrust of this book so far has been on manual technique. This chapter will deal with some of the musical and personal qualities needed to be a successful conductor, dwelling particularly on that aspect of personality called leadership.

MUSICAL QUALIFICATIONS

The musical qualifications of a good conductor include the following:

1. Musicianship. This means being sensitive to the expressive qualities as well as the technical aspects of music and being able to demonstrate that sensitivity via performance on one's major instrument or voice.
2. Having a mastery of baton technique so that one's musical conceptions can be efficiently and effectively conveyed to the ensemble. This includes proper use of the eyes and facial expression.
3. Understanding how to study and prepare scores properly and then do a thorough job of it. This includes the ability to sightsing individual parts and the ability to play from the score at the piano.
4. Knowing how to rehearse the ensemble so that every bit of rehearsal time is used to its best advantage and no time is wasted.
5. Having a solid background in music history and theory, including stylistic and formal analysis, in order to properly recreate the composer's ideas with musical integrity.

Item 1 (Musicianship) cannot be taught by a book. Item 2 (Mastery of Baton Technique) was the focus of the previous four chapters. Items 3 and 4 on score study and rehearsal procedure will be covered in Chapters 7 and 8. Item 5 will be discussed next in this section.

Historical and Theoretical Knowledge

The ultimate goal of conducting is to elicit a musically intelligent and enthusiastic performance from an ensemble. This is accomplished in part by the conductor's gestures, including not only the motions of the hands, arms, and torso, but also the information and emotion communicated through the eyes and facial expression. It also involves constantly listening to what is heard from the ensemble and comparing it to what is known and understood from the score.

With advanced ensembles in particular the conductor must be intimately familiar with the style of performance best suited to any given work. The foundation for this knowledge is developed in the study of music history and literature. Furthermore, through score preparation, the conductor must know not only the individual details—parts and sections of the score—but must also develop a clear conception of the complete work. This cannot be done without a sound knowledge of music theory, harmonic analysis, and musical form. A still broader picture of the work and its meaning may be gained from knowing its place among the composer's other works, the reason and occasion for its composition, the place and time of performance, and its relationship to other works of the period.

Such a broad picture cannot be expected of a beginning conducting student, but it is this depth of preparation that will eventually distinguish the individual who merely beats time while the group performs from the true conductor who can "bring a piece of music to life" for both the performers and the audience. This breadth of knowledge and skill allows the conductor more perfectly to match the sound coming from the group against the mental template she or he has of what the piece ultimately should be.

This depth of preparation cannot be provided in one or two conducting courses. Traditionally these content areas (theory, history, analysis, form) are covered in separate courses prior to or concurrent with the study of conducting. Because of this, beginning conductors tend to view the content areas as discrete packages of information with little direct relationship to each other. Often it is the conducting class that causes the student to integrate and synthesize this accumulation of skill and knowledge for the first time.

Conducting Musically

Although it is impossible to learn how to conduct musically through reading a book, there is one aspect of the topic that can be discussed beneficially in writing: the focus of one's attention during rehearsal and performance.

During outside practice sessions, conducting students should spend considerable time doing warmup exercises and working on technique. Vocal and instrumental performers do the same thing. But when it comes time to perform for others, the focus should be on musical expression, not conducting or performance technique. If you focus your attention on technique when conducting your ensemble, there is no way you can be a musically expressive conductor. Your manual technique may be flawless but musical expression will probably be lacking. The reason for this is that we function with one-track minds. We cannot concentrate fully on two activities simultaneously. Therefore, focus on technique during outside practice sessions; focus on the music itself during performance. As a conductor you are performing every time you stand in front of an ensemble. The ensemble may be practicing or rehearsing, but you should not be.

The preceding idea takes time for instructors to teach and for students to learn. The problem lies in clearly differentiating between the goals of outside practice and the goals of conducting/performing when in front of a live group. In simplest terms, the primary goals of outside practice should be to learn the music and to practice specific aspects of baton technique until they feel natural. When actually conducting a group, one should not be concerned with technique but should instead concentrate totally on expressing the music in one's head as well as possible, through well-learned baton and hand movements (as they exist in the subconscious mind). Compare this concept to performing expressively on your major instrument or voice. The performer cannot afford to think about the fingers, tongue, and other areas of technical function, all at the same time, and also play musically. In the same way, the conductor cannot concentrate on beat pattern clarity or some other aspect of baton technique and conduct musically, simultaneously. So, focus on the music alone during performance.

One bit of clarification is needed here. During rehearsals, the conductor must focus not only on the music but also on listening for performance problems. How can one do both? Actually one cannot do both very easily unless certain prerequisites have been met. The first of these is the working out and practice beforehand of baton techniques specific to the piece(s) being rehearsed. Second, a good, clear aural conception of the music needs to be acquired through intense, concentrated study of the score. Only then can the conductor give serious attention to rehearsal performance problems.

LEADERSHIP: THE ALL-IMPORTANT ABILITY

In outlining the personal qualities of a good conductor, one could list the attributes of a specific professional conductor who may be very dynamic, flambouyant, out-going, assertive, and yes, charismatic. These are the qualities that we frequently associate with "showmen" conductors. While each of these qualities is desirable so long as it is not overdone, we have found that one can be an effective conductor without possessing all of them. In fact it is possible to be a quiet, reflective, even introverted person and still be an effective conductor—if one possesses good leadership ability. But if the conductor lacks good leadership ability, no amount of other personality attributes can compensate or substitute. It is therefore our conviction that the most important personal qualification of a good conductor is that of leadership.

Given sufficient time plus correct study and practice, things like conducting technique, and requisite skills such as music theory, music history, and sightsinging can be learned. When it comes to acquiring leadership ability, the challenge is much greater; there is a certain intangibility to the quality of leadership. Because of this intangibility some believe that leadership cannot actually be taught, that leadership is based primarily on innate abilities. True, some people do seem to be "born leaders." Others seem to be "good, average, natural" leaders, while still others appear to be devoid of any kind of leadership ability. Despite these facts we believe that certain concrete aspects of the subject can be identified, analyzed, taught, and learned. The purpose of this section is to cover these aspects.

Leadership Defined

Leadership—what does it mean? To lead means to show the way by going before or in front of others; it means to serve as a guide. In dealing with a musical ensemble it means that from the moment that the conductor first steps on the podium, the performers will sense confidence level, level of preparation, musicality, and the degree to which she or he is "in charge." Some of the messages will be sent overtly by the way in which the conductor speaks, or by conducting gestures, and the confidence with which the rehearsal is carried out. Other signals will be sent through the subliminal messages transmitted by body posture, physical mannerisms, tone and volume of voice, facial expression, and particularly eye contact. Most of the "messages" that we send we can control with practice, and the first step in controlling them is simply to be aware that we are sending them.

The impression that the conductor creates on the podium, from both the content of the messages and the manner of delivery, will in large measure determine the success of his or her conducting and rehearsal efforts. This aggregate sense of preparedness, confidence, organization, and simply being in control of the situation is called leadership.

Types of Leaders

Essentially, there are two types of leaders: those who are basically authoritarian and those who tend toward being more democratic in style. Correspondingly, these types of leaders evoke two types of followers: (1)

those who follow their leader because they feel they have no other choice, and (2) those who are both willing and anxious to follow their leader because they respect and admire that person greatly. Both types of leaders are found among those who conduct musical ensembles, and it is likely that you have performed under at least one of each type. Consequently you may already have some very strong opinions regarding each of these types. You may also have a definite idea about the type of leader/conductor you want to be, but before you make a final irrevocable decision in this regard let us explore the subject further.

It has been said that the podium is the site of the last great dictatorship. However, we believe that with a few remaining exceptions the day of the authoritarian, tyrannical conductor is gone. It is no longer acceptable, even within professional ranks, for a conductor to impose his or her will in a militaristic, dictatorial fashion. But because this type of leader was accepted at one time in professional ensembles, this role model was also adopted by conductors in other areas, even those in educational settings. Today, however, most people (at least in this country) prefer to see themselves as the second type of leader—the one who is respected and admired by his or her followers.

Note that we used the words "respected" and "admired." We didn't say that the followers "liked" the leader; there is a real difference. The conductor first needs the respect of the ensemble. If their respect is earned, she or he will probably also gain their admiration. Eventually they may even learn to like a conductor, but that should not be one of your primary goals as their leader. If you try to get them to like you by being a "nice guy" or a "nice gal," you will probably never earn their respect or gain their admiration.

Leadership Characteristics

One of the primary leadership characteristics has already been identified, the ability to gain the respect and admiration of the ensemble. Another important characteristic is a sincere caring for the group and its members. In an ensemble, the welfare and best interest of the group should come before that of the conductor. Demonstrated enthusiasm by the conductor for improvement of the ensemble will also do much for developing positive morale. Once the performers see this happening, they too will be eager to make such a commitment. In this regard the use of positive reinforcement can be extremely beneficial. It is all too easy to move on to the next musical challenge in rehearsal without taking time to praise what has just been accomplished. If you and the performers have worked to achieve a particular musical result and have succeeded, make sure that they know you are pleased. Success in this area is built on sincere praise and encouragement, not constant criticism.

Conductors of school ensembles must combine the duties of preparing groups for concert and teaching them as well. This requires that they be both leaders and facilitators of learning. For the students to learn as effectively as possible they should be involved in making musical discriminations—discussing expressive possibilities such as phrasing, articulation, and dynamic contrasts. These decisions, normally made (dare we say dictated) by the conductor, can be shared with the student performers.

This may sound at first like we are advocating musical anarchy or some sort of participatory democracy with voting on proper tempo, dynamic levels, and so on. This is not the case. The conductor will in fact have to guide the students in discussing and evaluating the musical and expressive possibilities, and in most instances be the one who makes the final decisions. This is the responsibility of the school ensemble conductor.

Some aspects of leadership are based on appearance as well as attitudes. The way you look when you take the podium will say much about whether you are "in charge" or not. Take a firm, positive posture in your conducting and approach to the group. Speak so that all the performers can hear you easily, and with enough authority so that a "business-like" yet pleasant attitude can be created. As you address the group, make eye contact with the individuals to whom you are speaking. Nothing is quite as disconcerting as the conductor who talks into the score or stares above the heads of the performers while giving directions or making corrections. In other words, what we are talking about is conductor self-confidence, the subject of the next subsection.

Gaining Confidence and Earning Respect

A good leader must be confident and self-assured but without being arrogant. To gain confidence, conduct often. Conducting teachers are reminded that, especially during the early stages of learning, frequent short periods of time in front of a group are far better for most young conductors than long infrequent sessions.

Conducting time spent in front of an ensemble should consist mainly of positive experiences, not intimidating or degrading ones. In this respect, young conductors are often their own worst enemies. They fail to study their scores or prepare their conducting technique adequately. The result is embarrassment for all concerned. The greatest confidence builder is superior preparation. This means memorizing the score and being able to execute all of the necessary manual gestures properly. Hardly anything gains the respect of an ensemble more quickly than obvious superior preparation and execution by a conductor.

The ability to run a well-organized, efficient, and productive rehearsal is also important in earning the respect of an ensemble. A well-organized rehearsal is one that is well thought out beforehand and outlined in writing for reference during the rehearsal. Equally important is the ability to make sound musical and personal decisions in dealing with the performers. The rest depends on the conductor's knowledge, experience, and skill in rehearsal procedure. "A good conductor knows what she or he wants and knows how to get it" is another way of saying it. Also, a good conductor does not *demand* respect; it is given freely by the performers after it has been earned.

76　　Some conducting students work hard on both baton technique and score preparation yet still achieve mediocre results on the podium. When this happens, the frustration can be very great. Sometimes the problem is fairly easy to solve. On taking a very close look at the actual quantity and quality of preparation, we discover that what was originally perceived to be "working hard" really was not. Increased practice time and improved practice procedures are often all that is needed to improve conducting performance significantly. In other cases the problem goes deeper. The cause could be motivational (a lack of real interest in being a conductor) or it can be rooted in negative self-image (a low opinion of one's ability or potential for success).

If you happen to have a negative self-image, this is not terribly uncommon. A good number of people have this problem—and for no good, logical reasons. It is not an illness; it is based on what is almost always an erroneous attitude we have about ourselves or our abilities. Attitudes can be changed; the problem can be solved. (See Kohut's *Musical Performance*, pp. 43–46 and 135–141.)

Concluding Reminders

1. Thorough preparation is the key to leadership and self-confidence. If you make a mistake, admit it, correct it, and move on. Spending too much time apologizing and making excuses only places your insecurity on display.

2. Begin the rehearsal immediately after stepping onto the podium. If any explanation or opening comments are necessary, keep them brief and start making music. Time spent staring at the music and turning pages implies that you are still studying the score or are unsure of how to begin.

3. Speak with authority in a firm, distinct voice. This does not mean that you should speak loudly all the time; a soft voice also has its place. Make personal eye contact with the performers and communicate effectively. Directions mumbled with your head in the score will not be heard or followed.

4. Set high musical expectations for yourself and the group. Do not hesitate to correct errors made by individual performers, but do it tactfully. Avoid making an issue of obvious errors that will probably be corrected automatically the next time.

5. Above all, treat your performers with the same respect that you desire from them. Uphold their dignity as fellow human beings.

In the final analysis the four most important elements of conducting are leadership, musicianship, baton technique, and rehearsal effectiveness. Mastery of these elements is not accomplished merely by completing requisite classes or by the receipt of academic degrees. It is accomplished through an on-going process of study and reflection, observation and listening, creativity, experimentation, and expression. Without a life-long commitment to self-improvement, the conductor will stagnate and the ensembles she or he leads will not improve.

6 Clefs and Transposition

The purpose of this chapter is to provide requisite information that will allow the conductor to read and study an *instrumental score*. Understanding the various clefs used is the first step in this process. Knowledge of instrument transposition is the second essential step.

COMMONLY USED CLEFS

In this section only those clefs and instruments that are commonly used in today's bands and orchestras will be covered. This is done in order to keep the discussion as simple and concise as possible. Beginning and intermediate conductors, we believe, will find it adequate for their needs. More advanced conductors needing more comprehensive information will find it at the end of this chapter.

All band and orchestra instruments regularly use either the treble or bass clef except the viola which uses the C (alto) clef. The C (tenor) clef is used only in special cases as noted in Chart 1, on the next page. A quick way to transpose these clefs is as follows:

1. Alto clef is like treble clef *down* a tone.
2. Tenor clef is like treble clef *up* a tone.

CHART 1

G (treble) clef

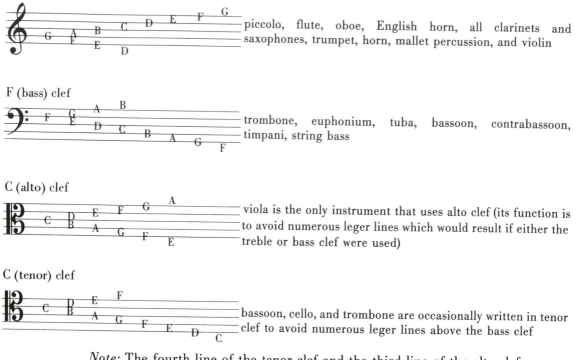

piccolo, flute, oboe, English horn, all clarinets and saxophones, trumpet, horn, mallet percussion, and violin

F (bass) clef

trombone, euphonium, tuba, bassoon, contrabassoon, timpani, string bass

C (alto) clef

viola is the only instrument that uses alto clef (its function is to avoid numerous leger lines which would result if either the treble or bass clef were used)

C (tenor) clef

bassoon, cello, and trombone are occasionally written in tenor clef to avoid numerous leger lines above the bass clef

Note: The fourth line of the tenor clef and the third line of the alto clef are equivalent to Middle C on the piano.

Exceptions to the classifications in Chart 1 are given below:

1. The euphonium is occasionally written in *treble clef* and treated as a B♭ transposing instrument sounding one octave below the B♭ trumpet. The purpose of the treble clef euphonium part is to facilitate player change-over from trumpet in school bands needing additional euphonium players.

2. The bass clarinet is occasionally written in *bass clef* and treated as a C-, B♭-, or A-pitched instrument. If indicated as bass clarinet in C, it is non-transposing. If indicated in B♭, the written notes sound a major 2nd lower. In A, they sound a minor 3rd lower.

3. The horn is also occasionally written in bass clef. According to Green, "When horn parts are notated in the bass clef, the transposition interval is the inversion of the interval in the treble clef." When this rule is not adhered to in modern practice, the composer usually so indicates in the score.*

*Elizabeth A. H. Green, *The Modern Conductor,* 4th ed, (Englewood Cliffs, NJ: Prentice-Hall, Inc., 1987) p. 143.

TRANSPOSITION DEFINITIONS

Concert pitch The pitch which actually sounds; the pitch as it exists on the piano.

Nontransposing instrument An instrument that requires no transposition; an instrument pitched in C (concert pitch).

Transposing instrument Any instrument whose written pitch sounds different from concert pitch and must be appropriately changed in order to be in unison with concert pitch.

Interval of transposition The pitch distance between concert pitch and where the instrument actually sounds.

Instrument pitch designation The pitch name assigned to a given instrument based upon its interval of transposition *away from* concert pitch, i.e., B♭ trumpet, F horn.

Sounding pitch The *actual* pitch that is heard/produced regardless of the note written for a given instrument; same as concert pitch.

Written pitch The pitch notated for a given instrument based upon its interval of transposition; the transposed pitch. (For nontransposing instruments, the written pitch and sounding pitch are the same, of course.)

The purpose of Example 25a and b below is to apply the information provided in the preceding definitions.

In Example 25a, the concert pitch C scale on the top stave is the same as a C scale on the piano. If a B♭ clarinet were to play this concert pitch C scale as written, the pitches notated in the second stave (which are a major second lower) would sound. Note that the key is also a major second lower (key of B♭). This means, first of all, that the B♭ clarinet is a transposing instrument. Its instrument pitch designation is B♭ because that is the pitch it sounds when the player *reads* concert C. And, finally, since it sounds a major second low to concert pitch, its interval of transposition is a major second up as seen in the third stave. These written pitches are what results from the transposition process. Note that the transposed key (D major) is also a major second up.

EXAMPLE 25.

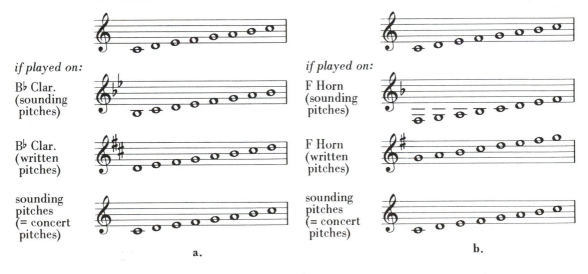

if played on:

B♭ Clar. (sounding pitches)

B♭ Clar. (written pitches)

sounding pitches (= concert pitches)

if played on:

F Horn (sounding pitches)

F Horn (written pitches)

sounding pitches (= concert pitches)

a.   b.

Example 25b gives another example, this one using the F horn. If an F horn were to play this concert pitch C scale as written, the pitches notated in the second stave (which are a perfect fifth lower) would sound. The F horn, therefore, is a transposing instrument. Its pitch designation is F because that is the pitch it sounds when the player *reads* a concert C. Since it sounds a perfect fifth low, its interval of transposition is a perfect fifth up as seen in the third stave. Note that the transposed key (G major) is also a perfect fifth up.

TRANSPOSITION PRINCIPLES

Young conductors sometimes find the transposition process difficult and confusing. If each instrument is dealt with as a separate, isolated entity, then the process can indeed be quite complex and confusing. To avoid this we recommend that the information be classified according to the various instruments' similarities and differences. Once the information is catalogued in the mind in this way, it is easier to retain and recall when needed. This does not mean it can be learned with minimal effort; lots of work is still needed. But we can promise that it can be learned faster and with less confusion than if each instrument were studied separately in isolated fashion.

The principles listed below, if memorized, will allow you to deal with all of the most common transposing instruments. Other, less common instruments are covered on page 83.

1. *All treble clef wind instruments* are transposing *except* flute and oboe which are pitched in C. *All* of them also *sound below* concert pitch *except* the E♭ soprano clarinet and C piccolo which sound a minor 3rd and one octave higher than written, respectively.
2. *All bass clef instruments* are nontransposing *except* the string bass which sounds one octave lower than written.
3. *All mallet percussion instruments* are non-transposing *except* xylophone and bell lyra which sound one octave higher than written and orchestra bells which sound two octaves higher than written. All are notated in treble clef.

Aside from the E♭ soprano clarinet, all of the exceptions cited above are treated essentially as nontransposing instruments by orchestrators and composers. The C piccolo, xylophone, and bell lyra are all written one octave lower than they sound in order to avoid using an inordinate number of leger lines above the treble staff. The string bass and contrabassoon are written one octave higher than they sound in order to avoid numerous leger lines below the bass staff. (There are exceptions to this generalization, notably in the scores of Richard Wagner. However, most orchestrators today seem to favor writing these parts "in the staff" as much as possible, presumably so that they will be easier to read.)

The part written for *actual* transposing instruments must be transposed in the opposite direction from the way the instrument sounds. This means that the E♭ clarinet, which sounds a minor third *above* concert pitch, must be written a minor third *below* concert pitch. Since all of the other transposing wind instruments *sound below* concert pitch, their written parts must be transposed *up* by an equivalent interval.

The only common instruments not covered in the preceding discussion are the violin, viola, and timpani, all of which are pitched in C and are nontransposing. The only thing to remember here is that the viola uses the alto clef.

Following is a table of transpositions for all of the common band and orchestra instruments. Note that the order in which the instruments are listed correlates with the three transposition principles cited earlier. Also note that instruments of the same pitch designation and the exact same transposition are grouped together for easier retention and recall.

TABLE OF TRANSPOSITIONS

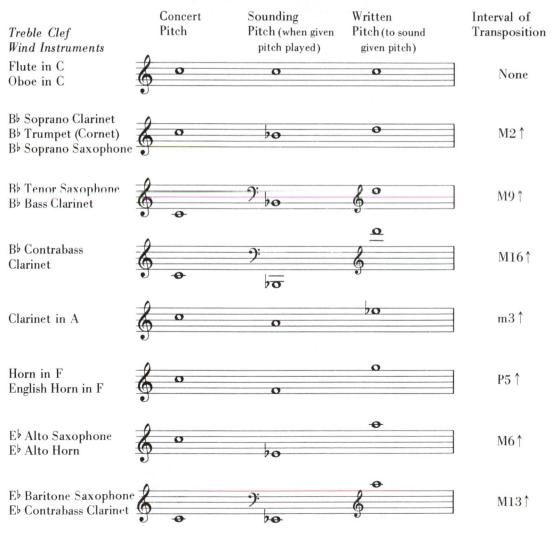

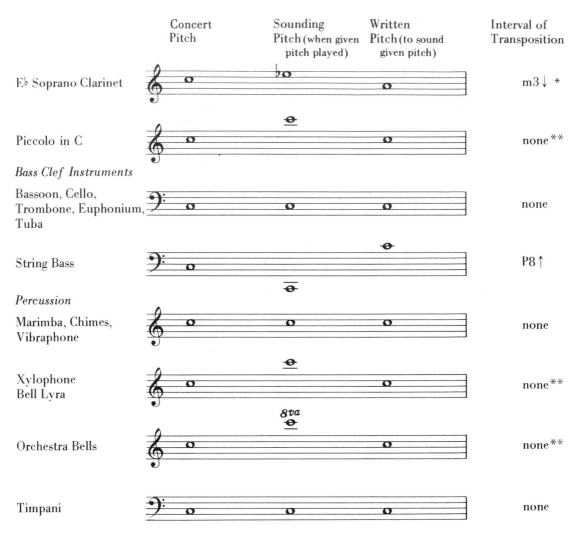

	Concert Pitch	Sounding Pitch (when given pitch played)	Written Pitch (to sound given pitch)	Interval of Transposition
E♭ Soprano Clarinet				m3↓ *
Piccolo in C				none**
Bass Clef Instruments				
Bassoon, Cello, Trombone, Euphonium, Tuba				none
String Bass				P8↑
Percussion				
Marimba, Chimes, Vibraphone				none
Xylophone Bell Lyra				none**
Orchestra Bells				none**
Timpani				none

*The E♭ soprano clarinet is the only transposing instrument on this chart which transposes down. All others transpose *up*.

**All of these instruments are treated as nontransposing in order to avoid numerous leger lines above or below the staff.

In reviewing the foregoing table, note the following:

1. All treble clef wind instruments are transposing except flute and oboe. All of them sound *below* concert pitch except the E♭ soprano clarinet and C piccolo.
2. All bass clef instruments are nontransposing except the string bass.
3. All percussion instruments are *treated essentially* as being nontransposing, regardless of the octave in which they sound.

Based on the above deductions, it is the treble clef wind instruments pitched in B♭, A, F, and E♭ that are the reason why this chapter needed to be written. The inevitable question at this point is *why*—why are most of the treble clef wind instruments transposing while the bass clef winds are nontransposing? It cannot be because of the instrument pitch designations; the trombone and euphonium are both pitched in B♭, yet they are nontransposing. We also have tubas pitched in BB♭, B♭, C, E♭, and F. One explanation is that the various sections of the orchestra were once *separate*, i.e., wind bands, church ensembles (trombones), and string orchestras. They each had their own unique ways of doing things which they *retained* even after being combined into the modern orchestra.

The next obvious question is why we do not change it? The answer is essentially the same as why we do not revamp the entire keyboard on the typewriter? What currently exists is not very good. Significant improvements need to be made to the typewriter keyboard and could easily be made by the manufacturers, but who is going to be the first to try it? The answer is no one. It is too big a change involving too many people and too much money. Therefore, we might as well accept the fact that instrument transposition, like the current typewriter keyboard, is here to stay, at least for quite a while longer.

Below is a list of transpositions for uncommonly-used instruments. Conductors working with more advanced instrumental ensembles will need to know these transpositions, of course, as well as the transpositions for the more common instruments discussed previously in this chapter.

Transpositions of Uncommonly-Used Instruments

Alto Flute in G	P4↑
Bass Flute in C	8ve↑
E♭ Flute	m3↓
E♭ Alto Clarinet	M6↑
Basset Horn in F	P5↑
A♭ Sopranino Clarinet	m6↓
Contrabassoon	8ve↑
B♭ Contrabass Clarinet	M16↑
B♭ Bass Saxophone	M16↑
D Trumpet	M2↓
E♭ Trumpet	m3↓
B♭ Piccolo Trumpet	m7↓
B♭ Bass Trumpet	M9↑
Euphonium (treble clef)	M9↑
B♭ Wagner Tuba	M2↑
F Wagner Tuba	P5↑

7 Music Selection, Score Study and Preparation

Before a lot of time is spent studying scores and preparing them for rehearsal, the conductor needs to be sure that the right music is selected—music that is right for the particular ensemble and music that is appropriate for the audience that will eventually be hearing it. This is why music selection is being discussed first in this chapter.

MUSIC SELECTION CONSIDERATIONS

The topics to be discussed in this section are (1) musical quality, (2) suitability for the ensemble, (3) programming considerations, and (4) the full versus the condensed score.

Musical Quality

The first and foremost criterion is that the literature selected be of good musical quality. This is quite obvious to most musicians, and yet we still find trite arrangements and synthetic ''pseudo-music'' being used in some school music programs. The usual justification given is that this music has value as ''training literature.'' We do not accept this as a valid justification. Rather we believe that music that is not worth performing for an audience is not worth doing in rehearsal or any place else. At the same time we do not mean that every piece selected should be a masterpiece comparable to Bach's B Minor Mass or Beethoven's Fifth Symphony. To the contrary, we simply mean that the music should possess expressive artistic qualities and be of aesthetic value to both performer and listener. To illustrate, some specific criteria are provided below.

Musical quality criteria

1. Has the work stood the test of time? This is a traditional criterion used by many music critics and one that obviously merits careful consideration by conductors.
2. Acknowledged quality of the composer or arranger. Although not every work by a good composer or arranger will be excellent, the majority usually are.
3. Expressive quality exemplified by musical tension and release. Music with expressive quality lends itself to being performed with feeling. Synthetic music is usually devoid of expressive content.
4. Closely related to Item 3 is the matter of expressive subtlety. Is the expressive quality of the music perceived after only one or two hearings, or does the music get better and better after each new hearing? Music well written will stand up well under close examination and analysis. It will reveal many possibilities for expressive nuance and will "wear well" in repeated rehearsals.
5. Good craftmanship. This simply means intelligent and skillful use of the musical elements along with appropriate scoring for the voices and/or instruments for which the work is intended.

The five criteria above should be viewed only as basic guidelines; they in no way provide a comprehensive view of this topic. The ability to select good music also involves far more than merely knowing a group of criteria. Ultimately the decisions you make must come out of your own informed musical judgment.

Suitability for the Ensemble

First, consider the purpose of the specific piece being chosen. Will it be used for sightreading, rehearsal and study, or performance? Pieces to be used for sightreading only should be easier than those chosen for performance, and occasionally it is worthwhile to rehearse and study a work which, because of its difficulty, may not be performed in public.

The question then is whether or not the difficulty of the music is compatible with your ensemble's performance skills? In other words, is it too easy, too difficult, or just right for the purpose intended? To determine this, you need to look at the following:

INSTRUMENTATION OR VOICING. The first page of a full score will include *all* of the instruments to be used in the piece, regardless of whether they play on the first note of the piece or not. Check to see if your ensemble has all of the instruments or voices required. In the case of choirs, are there enough singers within the sections to cover adequately the parts written, especially if there are divisi passages? If not, then is it possible or practical to rearrange the voicing? Usually the best solution is to search for another piece of music. The astute conductor will primarily choose music that emphasizes the strengths rather than the weaknesses of his or her group.

DIFFICULTY OF THE PART IN RELATION TO PERFORMER CAPABILITY. What musical difficulties does the work present in melodic and harmonic content, rhythm, tempo, and so on? Does it provide an appropriate level of challenge without being unreasonably frustrating? Student performers need a good mixture of levels of difficulty. Some pieces should be easily achievable so that immediate expressive results can take place. A few should be quite difficult and require a number of rehearsals to conquer and perfect, while most should fall in a medium category, presenting a balance of sections that are played with ease and those requiring more work.

Along with general musical characteristics, determine the difficulty level by checking these specifics:

1. Difficulty of the first trumpet (band), soprano (choir), or first violin (orchestra) parts. All too often these parts are written very high, making them one or even two grades higher in difficulty than all of the other parts. Unless you have very strong performers on these parts, this usually disqualifies such scores from performance consideration.
2. Playing ranges and the tessitura in which each part is written. Band and orchestra scores will not be written out of the range of a given instrument, but choral pieces may ask for pitches that the singers in your ensemble cannot produce comfortably. More important, if the part is written in an extreme tessitura for most of the piece, this may disqualify it for young performers.

WILL YOUR ENSEMBLE LEARN FROM AND ENJOY REHEARSING AND PERFORMING THIS PIECE? In other words, is the music (and text for choirs) compatible with the age level or musical maturity of your ensemble? If not, is there a good chance that you can guide them toward an understanding and appreciation of it through teaching, rehearsal, and analysis? Most important, will the students learn and grow as musicians from having rehearsed and performed this piece?

Programming Considerations

As stated above, the music chosen for rehearsal and performance needs to provide appropriate musical learning for student performers and be compatible with their interest and capability. Equally important is that the music be appropriate for the audience that will be hearing it. This does not mean that every piece programmed should be an "audience pleaser," but to ignore the kind of audience one will have and the context in which the performance takes place ("pops" concert or formal concert) would obviously be a mistake. How much new music should be programmed: serial, chance, aleatoric? How much popular music?

As both a teacher and conductor you must balance the need of your students to learn, against the audience's need for entertainment. There are no simple answers to these questions. You must use your own good musical judgment and common sense. At the same time remember that you reveal your competence as a musician in the music you use.

The Full Versus the Condensed Score

Another important consideration is the kind of score that is available—a full score, condensed score, or a piano-conductor? For choral ensembles the answer is simple: everyone reads from a full score. With instrumental ensembles, the ideal is to have a regular full score plus a two-stave condensed score written in concert pitch. The condensed score makes playing the score at the piano much easier. It also makes harmonic analysis easier and thus faster.

The two-stave condensed score is sometimes labeled "Piano-Conductor" even though it isn't necessarily written to be played at the piano. Sometimes the piano-conductor score is written on three staves. Condensed scores of four, five, or six staves with a different instrument family or melodic group scored on each stave also exist in some cases. All such condensed scores are usually in concert pitch. Full scores are usually transposed scores and will contain as many as twenty-five or more staves when written for symphonic band.

If a full score is not published and only a two- or three-stave condensed score is available, it makes serious score study and preparation difficult, unless the instrument cues are clearly labeled. If it is a rather complex piece, the absence of a full score makes study and preparation virtually impossible. One's only alternatives then are (1) to study each performer's written part carefully prior to the first rehearsal and hope for the best, or, perhaps more wisely, (2) not do the piece at all. Fortunately, most complex works do come with a full score. Less complex works, especially for young instrumental ensembles, are the ones with condensed score only.

BASIC SCORE STUDY SKILLS

"The score should be in your head, not your head in the score!" This directive is traditionally used by conducting teachers everywhere. Obviously it is a frequent and persistent problem. The two most basic skills needed by the conductor to solve this problem are sightsinging and piano skills.

Conductor Sightsinging Ability

Conductor sightsinging ability is important for two reasons: (1) as a primary means toward learning the score, and (2) as a primary approach to rehearsal procedure. If the conductor can sing each part and sing it musically, then he really knows each part. Once this has been accomplished, the conductor is then able to determine in rehearsal if the performers are performing the right notes in the proper way. If they are not, then the conductor's job is to *show them* how it should sound by singing it for them.

In a beginning conducting class, up to five minutes of each class period should be devoted to sightsinging, individually and collectively. The material used normally should consist of the scores assigned for a given class period. However, the instructor on occasion may choose to use actual sightsinging books if it is felt that the class as a whole needs additional intensive training in this area.

Piano Skills for the Conductor

The tasks of rehearsal demonstration and score preparation can be greatly enhanced and simplified if the conductor has good piano skills in addition to sightreading ability. For choral directors especially it is an *absolute must*. Rehearsal with school choruses cannot be accomplished without strong keyboard support. Since most school districts cannot provide a paid accompanist for every rehearsal and good student accompanists are not always available, the responsibility falls directly on the conductor's shoulders.

The choral teacher/conductor's responsibility is to be able to play well enough to supply: (1) an overview of each piece by playing through it, (2) harmonic support for rehearsal purposes, (3) a means of demonstrating and rehearsing multiple voice combinations for any and all parts, and (4) accompaniments (even if simplified) to enhance the expressive quality of choral performances. This is not meant to imply that the choral conductor should rely exclusively on the piano for rote teaching and voice part demonstrations. To the contrary, the teacher should model correct pitch, rhythm, tone, pronunciation, and expression by singing, but without strong keyboard skills, rehearsal efficiency will be greatly reduced.

Piano skills can also greatly aid score preparation for both instrumental and choral conductors. In addition to playing and singing through each individual part, much information and insight into compositional structure and rehearsal organization can be gained by playing each voice part in all possible combinations with the other parts (i.e., soprano/alto, soprano/tenor, soprano/bass, etc.). Piano skills can also help establish a clear concept of the harmonic content of the piece when recordings are not available. This cannot be accomplished by sightsinging.

GENERAL STUDY CONCEPTS

In studying a new score, first get an overview of the complete work—a sense of the "big musical picture." What do you know about the composer and his or her style? What is the form of the piece? Listen to some recordings, if any are available, or play through it on piano. Approach your study with the realization that eventually you will memorize the score. This is the only real solution to being able to keep your head out of the score *while* conducting. Central to the memorization process is repeated singing aloud of each line in the score and playing the full score at the piano as recommended earlier.

Initial Overview

The items below are listed in the general order in which they are to be studied. However, you may also choose to change the order because of the particular score you are studying. In the final analysis, the really important thing is that, by checking out each item individually, you will have gone through the complete score several times.

1. Who is the composer of this piece? What do you know about the composer and her or his compositional style and technique? If the composer is unknown to you, find out all you can through all of the resources available to you. (See the General Musical Texts listed in the Bibliography.)

2. What do you know about this piece? Was it written for any specific or special occasion? Are there any program notes available for study?

3. What kind of piece is this? Is it harmonic, contrapuntal, atonal? Are tone clusters and polychords used? Is your group capable of performing it?

4. What is the form of this piece? How do the various sections fit together? Is there a development section, a coda, an introduction, or transition sections? Now is the time to begin sketching these things out on paper. It is your first step toward eventual memorization. As you sketch, list the number of measures and the time signature in each section.

5. Locate the melodies and try to develop a feeling for correct tempi as soon as possible. This is critical because the tempi selected will directly affect the musical results of the work in all other respects including phrasing, style, and expression.

6. Find changes in key signature, tempo, and meter. Get a feel for the musical relationships of these variables. What kind of musical logic do you think the composer had in mind when using these variables in these particular ways?

7. Sightsing *aloud* each line of the score. If the score contains difficult wide intervals or is otherwise difficult to sightsing the first time through, then play each line on the piano or on your major instrument (transposed as needed). Each time afterward try to depend less and less on the use of an instrument as a crutch and more and more on your singing voice.

8. Play through all of the parts in combination on the piano. This provides the best overall concept of the piece. It should very definitely be done with choral scores and with condensed instrumental scores when available. Although more difficult to do with a full transposed instrumental score, the serious conductor will play at the piano, even if very slowly, all of the parts by instrumental section.

Listening to Recordings

An ideal way to learn how a piece sounds is to listen to one or more recordings of it, assuming these are available. This should be done both with and without the score. Without a doubt this process is much easier than studying the score alone and it also saves a great deal of time. A good recording also provides novice conductors with a good musical model to imitate while developing their own skills and repertoire. Would it not have been wonderful if the phonograph had been invented during Bach's time? It certainly would have eliminated most of the guesswork concerning matters of tempo, style, dynamics, and other factors, some of which still plague us today. Sound recordings, therefore, are a marvel of our century and we should not hesitate to use them to our advantage in learning musical scores.

We are very much aware, however, that there are those who are opposed to having student conductors rely on the use of recordings as described above. One common argument is that novice conductors who imitate the interpretation of the conductor on the recording will never develop their own interpretive skills. Another argument is that listening to recordings means that student conductors will never get around to detailed study of the score the way they should. We do not accept either of these arguments. In the first instance, there is nothing so terribly wrong with student musicians listening to and imitating acknowledged musical experts. Imitation is the most natural and efficient way that human beings learn and the learning of music is no exception in this regard. In the case of students neglecting proper score study when they listen to recordings, we are compelled to ask, "Isn't one of the prime purposes of score study to obtain an aural conception of the piece?" A good aural conception can, of course, be acquired through intensive study of the score alone. But if time can be saved by listening to a recording, if a more authoritative interpretation can be gained through listening to one or more recordings, we say do it.

When more than one good recording of a work exists, the conductor should definitely listen to them all. This is a very important part of the learning process. The more good music performed well that we hear, the better our musical conception. For conductors as well as individual performers, musical conception is *the first and foremost* aspect of musical performance!

Obviously the best way to acquire good musical conception is to attend live concerts and recitals, and we strongly recommend this as a basic component of every musician's training. This discussion on recordings is included only because of the greater accessibility provided by recordings when studying specific scores.

Memorizing the Score

Score memorization is very important, yet the conductor should realize that memorizing the score does not necessarily mean one should *conduct* without a score. While some conductors do conduct without a score, most conductors use the score during performance mainly as a reference. Therein lies the key—using the score as a reference. Refer to the score when needed but do not rely on it constantly. This applies as much to rehearsal as it does to concert performance. Having the score available for reference during the concert helps avoid the conductor's nightmare of getting lost in the middle of a piece. Trying to conduct without a score and getting lost proves nothing positive.

Conducting students sometimes use the score as a kind of "security blanket," that is, they put their heads down and look at it simply because it is there. Most of the time they do not really need to do this since they know their score fairly well, but they watch it anyway. Obviously this is a terrible habit and can be very difficult to eradicate. We believe that, ultimately, the best solution is to prevent its being learned. From the start, beginning conductors should be required to conduct without a score. Using the relatively short musical excerpts in Part II of this text makes this goal a practical one. With practice, it becomes easy eventually to conduct longer pieces without a score. The end result should be the desired one: conductors who use the score for reference but do not depend on it while conducting and rehearsing.

Listed below are other positive outcomes from having the score memorized:

1. Eye contact can be maintained with the ensemble. The expressive and personal communication made with the eyes is as important as the physical gestures made with the hands.

2. The conductor can concentrate on leading the ensemble instead of following it. When good eye contact is evident, the performers are more apt to *let* the conductor lead them.

3. The conductor can concentrate more on the musical images in the mind's ear and more readily express them via hand gestures. During rehearsal it is also easier to listen and actually hear the ensemble. This allows for more effective and efficient rehearsal procedure.

4. Perhaps most important is the confidence the conductor can feel in front of an ensemble when he or she really knows the music, and the musical thrill experienced when one is not burdened by the score itself.

DETAILED SCORE STUDY

It is very easy to be complacent, to do only the initial overview steps outlined earlier and let that suffice for the first rehearsal. Conductors who do this usually do not prepare much for succeeding rehearsals either; they simply try to learn the music during rehearsals with the ensemble. Obviously this is not recommended. It is often acceptable and appropriate for the performers to be sightreading a new piece of music in rehearsal, but not the conductor. The conductor should know the entire score well. The following is a discussion of what should be studied before the first rehearsal and how to go about it.

Establishing the Correct Tempo

The conductor's first responsibility is to establish the correct tempo. An incorrect tempo can destroy the music from an expressive standpoint. Performing a piece at the wrong tempo can also disguise the musical style and even the composer in some cases. It simply should not be done.

How does one determine the correct tempo for a given piece? First, the conductor needs to be as familiar as possible with the composer and his or her music. If a metronome marking is available, this certainly helps, but the conductor still needs to be familiar with the composer's musical style since this helps the musical ear to decide when the tempo feels right. When metronome markings are not provided, then the conductor alone must make the choice or consult a recording, if one is available. Then he or she needs to try various tempi that are slightly slower and slightly faster than the recording to decide which feels best. (The metronome marking is usually meant to be a general guide, not an absolute rule.) As part of this process, the conductor should learn to sing each line so that it can be modelled correctly when rehearsing the ensemble; i.e., use of correct diction for singers, correct tonguing syllables for wind players, proper bowings for strings. Be sure to do all of this *aloud*. One only learns what one actually does.

Melody

Having located the actual melodies earlier, now is the time to do phrase analysis and work on melodic interpretation. Where do the phrases begin and end? What are the primary notes toward which the secondary notes "travel"? What about phrasing in general? What is needed to make the phrasing musical within the context of the composer's style? How do the individual phrases fit together—into a period, section, a complete theme?

With choral music, consideration also must be given to how the musical phrases are combined with the lines of text. In some cases the punctuation or sentence structure will not correspond exactly with the musical phrasing, and a compromise must be reached. The combination of word and syllabic stress should be integrated with the musical goals to establish the expressive content of the work.

Usually the melody is fairly easy to locate, but obbligato lines and melodic derivations may not be discovered as easily. (By melodic derivations we mean short imitative motifs and melodic fragments which may or may not be related to the principal melody.) Once these have been located, bracket them in the score so you can easily find them next time.

Related to the preceding discussion is the fact that good composers and arrangers usually make a conscious effort to make the bass line and inner parts interesting musically. They do this by thinking horizontally (melodically) as well as vertically (harmonically). (J.S. Bach's chorales are an outstanding example of this idea.) When this is done, it makes the nonmelody parts more musical and much more satisfying for the performers. Look for this kind of writing when studying scores and emphasize it in rehearsal. Also look for it when selecting new music for purchase.

Harmony

In studying the harmonic and contrapuntal aspects of a given score, the following specific items should be considered:

1. How is the work supposed to sound? Chordal analysis using roman numerals may be helpful, but most important is the big aural picture. This is especially important regarding complex sections which are not easily deciphered aurally merely by looking at the score. Such sections in particular should be carefully analyzed and played at the piano until you get the sound in your "mind's ear."

2. As the chords of the work are played, the conductor should also sing through each chord from bottom to top so that he or she can eventually audiate or inwardly hear each progression even when there is no sound. This musical memory or ability to create the sound of the work in the mind's ear is an absolute necessity so that the conductor can reproduce accurately the sounds of the musical symbols in performance.

As stated earlier in this chapter, playing each part in combination with all other parts will provide a clear picture of the harmonic and structural organization of the piece.

Rhythm

Rhythm is the main element which creates musical movement and motion. This is true even in music designed for performance at a very slow tempo. Therefore, we need to determine how this motion is to be achieved in given musical works.

In our system of rhythmic notation for instrumentalists, beams are used to organize divisions and subdivisions of the beat into rhythmic groups. These allow the player to determine quickly where the beats occur, the number of notes within each beat, and the distribution of these notes within the beat. While this system is very logical and useful from the standpoint of music reading per se, it does not give any clues regarding the musical motion that given rhythmic patterns are supposed to initiate. If the rhythmic beam is interpreted literally with the performers emphasizing the first note of each beamed group as shown in Example 26a, the result will be a mechanical, nonmusical performance. If, on the other

EXAMPLE 26.

a.

b.

hand, the notes are grouped with musical motion in mind as shown in Example 26b, then we will have achieved a musical interpretation which allows the line to move and to sing.

Once these and other related questions have been answered, then be prepared to demonstrate your concept of the music vocally to the performers. Obviously this topic is a study in itself and beyond the scope of this book; we recommend the following three books as initial references to be read. Additional references are found in the Bibliography.

BARRA, DONALD. *A Dynamic Performance: A Performer's Guide To Musical Expression and Interpretation.* Englewood Cliffs, NJ: Prentice-Hall, 1983.

KOHUT, DANIEL L. *Instrumental Music Pedagogy.* Englewood Cliffs, NJ: Prentice-Hall, 1973. Chapter Five: Phrasing and Interpretation.

THURMOND, JAMES MORGAN. *Note Grouping: A Method for Achieving Expression and Style in Musical Performance.* P.O. Box 603, Camp Hill, PA: JMT Publications, 1982.

Marking the Score

How does one properly mark a score? Some believe the answer is *do not* mark it at all. We have all seen scores with so many markings on them that the notes can hardly be seen anymore. Others contain large sweeping lines and huge personalized symbols that are also distracting to the next conductor who tries to use the same score. On the other hand, there are some score markings that are valuable and most appropriate. We simply need to be judicious and limit our markings to those that are genuinely valuable.

When markings are made in the score, they should be there mainly to help one *study and learn the score,* not to be used as a "crutch" *while conducting.* These markings might include an arrow pointing toward an entrance which needs to be cued, the use of brackets to highlight an important inner part which needs to be brought out, or circling a subito piano dynamic marking or an isolated accent which could be easily overlooked. Again the underlying purpose should be to aid the conductor in the *study* of the score. The markings should not be there to help the conductor keep his or her place while watching the score in rehearsal or, even worse, during the performance.

While we obviously take a rather conservative view toward the marking of scores, other authors like Elizabeth A.H. Green and Nicolai Malko take a more liberal view, including use of different colored pencils for different dynamics. Those interested in more detailed information on this topic are advised to refer to their writings listed in the Bibliography.

Text: *Pronunciation and Meaning*

An added responsibility in preparing choral works is determining the pronunciation and meaning of the text. With texts in English, standard pronunciations may need to be somewhat modified for vowel purity, tonal coloring, and placement within the vocal range. When foreign language texts are used, as they frequently are, the conductor must check in advance any pronunciations which may come into question on a specific work.

The conductor must also consider how the text fits with the music of the piece. Careful attention should be given to phrase length and articulation for breathing. Without such planning, both tone quality and intonation will suffer.

Further, it is our belief that some general consensus should be reached between the conductor and performers regarding the meaning of the text to be sung. In some instances the text will be straightforward and not need interpretation. In many other cases, however, the poetry used will have less obvious meanings and be open to interpretation. While it may not be possible to reach complete agreement on what a particular text means, it will greatly enhance the performance if the conductor and performers have shared in a discussion of the meaning of the text and the composer's intentions for expressing it.

Marking Bowings and Articulations

Bowing and articulation is a complex subject in itself and will not be discussed in detail here. Suffice it to say that it is a subject of great importance to conductors since they must be prepared to edit bowings and articulations in the individual parts when this has not been adequately done in the published edition. This is particularly true in the case of the string bowings. For a general orientation to this subject, read Chapter Four of Kohut's *Instrumental Music Pedagogy*, published by Prentice Hall, plus the other references listed in the Bibliography. This should be followed immediately with live demonstrations in class by a string player and a wind player going through each of the various bowings and articulations available.

Other Study Items

1. Identify the dramatic content of the work. Determine what the various dynamic contrasts are and where they exist. Locate the climax(es). Note stylistic contrasts, changes in tempo and meter. With choral works, look for important words, and phrases that should be emphasized as well. In other words, understand what dramatic devices there are in the piece which will make the music alive and exciting for the audience.

2. Are any special effects employed in this work? This includes use of harmonics on string instruments plus muting, sul ponticello (on the bridge), and other devices. Use of mutes for brass instruments should also be carefully checked. What is the specific effect desired? Which mute will best achieve that effect, if not clearly marked in the part? Then there is the whole area of multiphonics and other devices for woodwind instruments used by contemporary composers. With contemporary choral works, identify any unusual vocal sounds and the symbols used to notate them. Finally, the availability of numerous types of sticks for playing

the mallet percussion instruments allows for a plethora of different tonal colors and dynamics. School music directors in particular need a thorough knowledge of this area.

MANUAL TECHNIQUE DECISIONS

Each piece of music has its own unique characteristics and the conductor must be ready to deal with them. The most common questions that usually arise in this regard are (1) Which voice part should I conduct? (2) How many beats should I conduct in each measure? and (3) When should I use divided beats? In addition, each piece will contain its own set of demands and challenges, calling for specific manual gestures that will require special emphasis in daily warmup and practice. Finding answers to these questions is the purpose of this section.

Which Voice Part Should I Conduct?

If all parts are notated in the same rhythm, then you can conduct all of the parts simultaneously. Frequently, however, the various voice parts employ diverse rhythms and possess melodic and harmonic functions that are equally diverse. Given this situation, it is obvious that the conductor cannot realistically conduct all of the parts at once. Those who try end up being little more than human metronomes. The solution in this case is to conduct only the most important part. Usually this is the melody. Sometimes the melody line can easily carry itself, not requiring any major input from the conductor, while a counter-melody needs special attention. There will be other instances where special effects merit special attention. An example of this might be a short staccato or heavily accented accompaniment line underlying a strong legato melody. A highly syncopated obbligato may likewise take precedence over a melodic line consisting mainly of long tones. In each case the choice that needs to be made will be fairly obvious. If in doubt, try it both ways in rehearsal and then decide.

If most of the conductor's attention is focused on conducting the melody, what do the performers on the other parts do? They should listen to the melody and support it in an accompanying way. They should also listen carefully to each other in order to maintain good rhythmic precision and motion, plus good intonation, balance, and tonal blend.

There may be some who have just read the above with some degree of disbelief. How can a conductor afford to ignore two-thirds to three-fourths or more of the ensemble performers, while conducting mainly a single voice line like the melody? First of all, the conductor does not ignore entirely those players or singers with supporting voice parts. One simply does not give them the same degree of attention as is given to the melody. But the main thing that we believe some conductors need to come to terms with is that they are not as essential to a group's performance as they sometimes think they are. They tend to take themselves too seriously. They think they have to indicate every beat, every nuance, every cue for every performer. They appear to believe that the ensemble simply cannot function without their presence on the podium. Without a doubt, a good teacher/conductor is essential in rehearsal situations in order to "whip a group into shape." In the concert performance situation someone is also needed to start and stop the ensemble, and negotiate fermatas and tempo changes. Good conductors also communicate musical style, dynamics, accents, and other expressive aspects of the music. At the highest level a good conductor is able to elicit musical responses from the ensemble which seem spontaneously inspired. But one thing no ensemble needs is a time-beater, someone who functions like a human metronome that you wind up for each piece. Certainly this is true for musical forms such as marches and short dance movements. It is equally true for many individual steady tempo sections in larger musical works as well. The conductor's role is to lead the ensemble musically, to really make a difference in how they sound. While it is a basic fundamental, time-beating is one of the least important things a good conductor does.

How Many Beats Should I Conduct in Each Measure?

In $\frac{4}{4}$ meter, should I beat four or two? In $\frac{2}{4}$ should I beat two or one? Should I beat six or two in $\frac{6}{8}$? These are typical questions the conductor must answer while studying and preparing the score. They are also very significant concerns because an error in judgment can have very direct and adverse effects on the musicality of the performance.

First of all, the tempo chosen by the conductor directly affects the number of beats to be used. So will the musical style, in some cases. There will also be times when the conductor should change back and forth from two to four beats per measure or from two to one, depending mainly on style changes. Typically a highly rhythmic section might best be conducted in four and an ensuing long tone legato section be conducted in two in order to achieve better musical flow. Beyond these general suggestions it is not possible to be more specific. Each piece is somewhat different, and will need to be viewed with "fresh eyes," with decisions made on an individual basis based upon the conductor's musical sensitivity. This will evolve as a result of repeated singing and playing of the melodic line in order to decide precisely what makes the most musical sense. Once the tempo and style are clearly established, deciding how many beats to conduct per measure becomes possible.

The usual problem that novice conductors have in this area is that they choose to beat fast 6, 4, or 2 when they should be beating a slow 2 or 1. The result is a heavy, cumbersome, draggy performance. When the conductor's beats are heavy and cumbersome, the ensemble performers directly reflect that. Usually the performance problem can be quickly solved simply by having the conductor cut in half the number of beats and decrease the size of the pattern.

In conclusion may we suggest that the very beginning of a piece or specific section or movement does not always give the best clue to the correct tempo. You may need to check other phrases further into the piece to get the correct feel for the tempo.

When Should I Use Divided Beats?

The answer is that divided beats should be used when they are needed to maintain good rhythmic movement and clarity in the piece. Tempo indicators like Grave and Lento usually require a divided beat pattern, but not always. Use divided beats only when necessary.

Realize that once you decide to use a divided beat pattern, you do not have to use it in every measure or for every beat. The rhythms used and the precise content of the musical line will determine what is needed at any given moment. Here, as in all other aspects of conducting, we must remain flexible and base our decisions on musical sensitivity and performance logic. The only genuine rule to follow is that the result should be a musically intelligent and enthusiastic performance.

Practice Exercises for Specific Works

Each work contains its own set of demands and challenges with regard to manual technique. For example, one piece may require a weighted gesture and frequent use of the left hand for indicating crescendi and decrescendi. Another work may contain complex changing meters along with frequent cuing of individual entrances. Whatever the requirements may be, we recommend that you create exercises for daily practice that are designed to habituate the skills involved. Outline these exercises on paper first, and then commit them to memory so they can be drilled by rote.

In school situations conductors have the opportunity to practice manual technique exercises with the ensemble during the tuning and warmup period. Memorized scales in particular lend themselves perfectly to most such exercises. Below are some examples of specific ways that scales can be used for this purpose. Create similar exercises on your own based on the needs of a particular score.

EXAMPLE 27.

Up to this point we have dealt exclusively with the musical elements of score study and preparation plus related manual technique considerations. For the conductor of a professional ensemble, this is normally all that is needed. If one is a conductor of school ensembles, however, one must also be prepared to deal with problems in performance technique and fundamentals of musicianship. For this reason the focus of this chapter will now shift to the kinds of problems one can expect to encounter with school ensembles.

Introduction

One measure of a successful teacher/conductor is the ability to teach difficult music to inexperienced performers. It is not merely the ability to "pound it into them" through repetition; it is more the art of unlocking the puzzles of complex musical writing. The first step toward this goal is careful and thorough score study. If the conductor knows the score intimately, many of its mysteries will solve themselves.

The manner in which the music is rehearsed will also have a telling effect on how much is accomplished. Score study will reveal what the core or central concept of a composition is. It may be primarily melodic in nature, or, in another case, it may be centered on rhythmic interest with little melodic writing at all. This central concept should be the foundation of the conductor's rehearsal planning. It should be used as the key to unlock the other elements.

One's ability to anticipate specific performance problems is directly related to the amount of practical knowledge and experience one has. The greater the knowledge and experience, the better the ability to anticipate the problems.

Obviously practical experience cannot be bought, nor can it be acquired via class discussion or reading a book like this one. It is acquired through being confronted with the actual problems in live rehearsal situations. But first one needs at least to be aware of the kinds of problems that one can expect to encounter. These include pitch and rhythmic reading, intonation, key changes, fingerings (including alternates) for instrumentalists, pitch placement for singers and brass players, tone production, and response problems. In addition, be ready to explain how to perform any trills, appogiaturas, mordents, or other ornamentation in the piece along with any special fingerings needed. With singers, plan to spend time in each rehearsal on maintaining correct pitch level.

Coping with a Condensed Instrumental Score

If the only score available is a condensed one, the conductor has two alternatives: (1) to study each performer's written part carefully prior to the first rehearsal, or (2) not do the piece at all. Assuming a decision is made to do the piece, then the study of each written part must be focused on learning it completely. Once the parts are distributed, the learning of them is finished.

With school instrumental groups, learning the parts completely means at least simulated playing through each part on the instrument for which it was written. In the process the conductor needs to make notes of all anticipated player problems. The younger the players, the more detailed and numerous the notes will need to be. The same holds true for school choral groups. The conductor must also be a teacher in the complete sense of the word. Since a comprehensive analysis of vocal and instrumental technique problems is beyond the scope of this book, we refer you to the Bibliography which lists many fine treatises on these topics.

Brass Instrument Pitch Placement

With school groups, be prepared to sing the starting pitches for the horns. In a regular full score they will be written a perfect fifth above concert pitch. Do not try to transpose their notes back to concert pitch and then try to sing their pitches. Instead, sing the chord root in concert pitch to yourself. Then look at the horn parts, determine the note that is the chord root in their key. Let your root be the root in their key (see Example 28).

This approach has worked well for many of our students. We hope it works well for you. If you have perfect pitch, the process will probably be more confusing than helpful. In any case, find some kind of system that works for you. At least some, if not all, of your horns will require your assistance in this area.

While correct pitch placement is uniquely more difficult on horn, younger players on the other brasses will also have their share of pitch placement problems. A recommended solution is to start each piece in rehearsal by saying, "Play your first note as a long tone." This allows the conductor to determine who needs help right from the start. Once everyone is playing the correct partial, then the group is ready to begin playing the piece.

Other Concerns

WHERE TO BREATHE. The obvious place for singers and wind players to breathe usually is at the ends of phrases, but not always! If continuous

EXAMPLE 28.

First chord
of work in
concert pitch

Horn
parts

Think:
3rd
root
5th
root

Sing the root, 5th, root, 3rd using the pitches in your ear based on concert pitch.

sound is desired through the individual phrases, then staggered breathing needs to be used. This is a decision that should be made prior to the first rehearsal. If staggered breathing is to be used, the ensemble should be so informed before they sing or play the first note.

PERCUSSION CUES.   The cues the conductor gives to the percussion players are among the most important cues given. Percussionists often must enter after a very long rest and, for this reason, especially need to be cued. Cymbal crashes should always be cued and circled in red in the score. Timpani should also be cued, especially in loud entrances. With younger players, the conductor should listen very closely for accurate timpani pitches when the player must retune *during* the piece itself.

INTONATION.   In harmonic music the bass voices set the tuning standard since they are the main ones sounding the roots of the chords. Therefore, begin by trying to anticipate intonation problems in the bass line since these will affect the entire ensemble. With wind instruments and the strings, look for typical "bad notes" which appear as long, sustained notes in the score. These notes will surely create at least minor intonation problems, if not major ones.

BALANCE OF THE PARTS.   The melody is normally thought of as the most important part. Second in importance is the bass part and then the inner parts. Since the melody is the most important part, it must be heard. Check the scoring to see if this will be easily accomplished and, if not, decide how to achieve desired balance through changes in instrumentation or number of performers on given parts.

CHORDAL BALANCE.   In tertian harmony the root is the most important, then the third. Next comes the seventh (if there is one), and then finally the fifth which is the least important and may even be omitted occasionally. In quartal harmony, tone clusters, and polychords, each note is of equal importance and must be equal in loudness. Otherwise the sound will be strange; something will sound wrong.

In closing we wish to point out that the key to good score study is to study your scores every day. Each new day delve into them more deeply and really learn (memorize) them. Trying to learn a full score overnight or in two or three days is just as bad as trying to cram for a written examination. Instead, the information found in a musical score needs to be digested, gestated, incubated, and absorbed over a relatively long period of time.

8 *Rehearsal Procedures*

Simply stated, rehearsal procedures are methods of teaching used in ensemble rehearsals. They are used to improve and refine ensemble performance skills such as attacks, releases, and musical expression. They are also used to communicate technical and musical concepts that cannot be conveyed with hand gestures and facial expression, such as intonation, balance, and blend.

After discussion of some preliminary items, this chapter deals with the structure and content of the rehearsal: warmup and tuning, the rehearsal proper and its focus on the synthesis-analysis-synthesis approach, rehearsal priorities, error detection, pacing, and other related matters. This is followed by a section called "Rehearsal Teaching and Evaluation," covering performance fundamentals like music reading and intonation, plus taping of rehearsals for evaluation purposes. The chapter ends with a discussion of choral standing arrangements and their effect on intonation, tone quality, balance, and blend.

PRELIMINARY CONSIDERATIONS

Three preliminary items will be considered here, the first of these being ensemble performance level. In plain words, do you conduct a professional ensemble, or do you work with a variety of school groups? The answer here has a direct influence on the second item, rehearsal goals, which in turn directly affects the third, prerehearsal planning. Prerehearsal planning is the crucial first step toward an efficient, productive rehearsal.

Ensemble Performance Level

When conducting a professional ensemble, rehearsal activities are usually directed exclusively toward performance preparation. If the group is a school ensemble, activities related to musical learning and improvement of technique must be included in addition to performance preparation. In the latter case, the conductor is also a teacher and, therefore, must assume a dual responsibility.

Rehearsal and learning goals also vary depending on the grade level and experience level of the students involved. Members of beginning groups should spend more time on improving tone quality, music reading, performance technique, and development of general musicianship, rather than preparing numerous performances. With these groups, performance can be used as an incentive for technical and musical improvement. As the students improve and acquire more skills and knowledge, public performance can take on a more important role. In advanced school groups (after appropriate learning and development have taken place), high quality performance eventually becomes a primary goal and the rehearsal becomes the means toward achieving it.

Rehearsal Goals

One goal of rehearsal is to work on those aspects of performance that cannot be communicated via hand gestures and facial expression. These include music reading, intonation, tone quality, balance, and blend—all of which must be carefully checked individually. Especially when working with school groups, the conductor will also need to correct wrong pitches and rhythms, as well as articulation, bowing, and diction. With professional ensembles, time will probably be devoted primarily to the refinement of musical expression and ensemble precision.

Now let us discuss what *should not* be done in rehearsal. First of all, do not waste time telling the performers to crescendo in bar two and diminuendo in bar three when your right hand beat pattern does not change in size and your left hand is immobile at your side. Second, do not yell at the group to sing or play softly when your beat size clearly indicates a forte dynamic level. Both of these examples represent an inexcusable waste of valuable rehearsal time. The point we wish to make here is that a good rehearsal conductor relies first on conducting techniques to convey her or his musical intentions. If a crescendo and diminuendo is desired, this should be clearly indicated with the hands. If a soft dynamic is desired, use a small beat. In other words, *show* them how with your hands; avoid *telling* them anything that can be easily communicated with the hands.

There will be times when you clearly indicate with your hands exactly what you want but the ensemble fails to respond in kind. As an initial step, stop and ask them to *watch* you more carefully the second time. Teach them to be more observant. We believe this is better than telling them immediately *what* they failed to see and *what* you want them to do.

There will also be times when you want to specify a precise amount, degree, or level that you want of a given musical element. You may be using a small beat, the ensemble is performing softly, but you want it "softer still" or "just a *little* louder." In such a case, words can be very helpful; conducting gestures alone may not be enough. But we urge you to remember that superior rehearsal conductors talk very little in rehearsal. When they stop the ensemble, most of the time is spent modeling what they want with their singing voice. The main words good conductors use are: softer, louder; faster, slower; shorter, longer; higher, lower (in pitch); brighter, darker (in quality).

Prerehearsal Planning

Efficient planning and organization are essential to the success of any activity. This is especially true of activities involving large numbers of people in complex procedures, such as music learning and rehearsals. Well-organized rehearsals based on clearly defined short- and long-term learning and performance objectives result in musically educated students and superior performances. To meet the immediate needs of beginning conducting students, most of the rehearsal goals in this chapter will focus on performance related materials.

Planning for any rehearsal should begin with a consideration of the following factors:

1. The reading and performance abilities of the group.
2. The difficulty and amount of music to be rehearsed.
3. The time available for rehearsal—both length of rehearsal periods and the total number of rehearsals before a performance.

It is readily apparent that the three factors cited are interdependent and adjustments in one area can overcome deficiencies in another. Beginning performers will need more time to learn difficult music than advanced; difficult music can be done with *more* time, and so on. This may appear to be *very* obvious, but much time and effort can be wasted if you choose music that is too difficult for the performers or too extensive for the relatively small amounts of time available in conducting class.

The second stage of prerehearsal planning should include the following:

1. Know you score as well as possible. This is the most obvious, yet most important factor.
2. Have a specific rehearsal plan written out beforehand. Know exactly what you intend to do and what you can reasonably expect to accomplish.

3. For ensemble and self-evaluation purposes, record each rehearsal, on audio tape at least, but preferably on video tape.

4. Review the tape of the most recent rehearsal before making plans for the next rehearsal.

Structuring the rehearsal by careful prerehearsal planning cannot be overemphasized. Valuable time is wasted and performer confidence lost if the rehearsal begins with the conductor shuffling through his or her folder and then asking, "What shall we start with today?" A very clear, well-organized rehearsal plan is necessary to accomplish desired performance and learning goals, to build good work habits and to develop positive attitudes toward the rehearsal itself.

THE WARMUP AND TUNING PERIOD

In all except the most advanced or professional ensembles, each rehearsal should begin with a warmup and tuning period. It is especially important for younger performers in training ensembles. The purposes of this period and recommended strategies for its efficient use are covered in the following subsections.

The Purposes of Warmup

There are three purposes of warmup. First of all, since the warmup period is literally the first playing or singing of the day for the students, the body parts used (the lips, tongue, arms, vocal cords, fingers, breathing muscles) must be limbered up and made ready to perform. Since singing and playing in vocal and instrumental ensembles are very physical activities when done properly, the body must be awakened and literally warmed up if ideal results are to be achieved.

Warmup also serves as a focusing event. In school ensembles the performers will all be coming from different classes and activities. Warmup can help focus each performer's attention on the musical exercises at hand. The concentrated effort needed to meet the goals of a disciplined warmup period can provide a strong positive beginning to the rehearsal period as a whole.

What should the performers concentrate and focus on? First, they should concentrate on listening—to intonation, balance, blend, attacks, and releases. Second, they should concentrate on watching—the conductor, for changes in tempo, dynamics, and style. The goal is to establish good listening and watching habits that will carry over into the regular rehearsal period.

Finally, the warmup period can function as a group technique lesson. Few school ensembles are so fortunate as to have all or even a majority of their members studying privately. The responsibility of teaching them how to play and sing properly is the conductor's. With careful planning the warmup can serve as a brief technique lesson where the students concentrate on developing tone quality, flexibility, dexterity, and range expansion. During the warmup period, the conductor can also develop the group's ability to listen for and achieve blend, balance, and good intonation within and between the sections.

Warmup Exercises

As we said, the performers should concentrate in two areas during warmup—listening and watching. To best accomplish this, the warmup exercises should be memorized. For instrumental groups, major and minor scales are used most often. These can be varied rhythmically for added interest, and a variety of articulations and bowings can also be used as needed.

Various exercises can also be created with memorized chords. One is to play or sing a series of chords upward chromatically and back down. Another is to lower the third of a major chord to make it minor, raise the fifth to make a major chord augmented, lower both the third and fifth to produce a diminished chord. In addition to intonation, chord exercises are especially good for checking balance and blend.

To work on attacks and releases, do some preparatory-attack-cutoff sequences as prescribed in Chapter 1. Also practice inhaling with your performers during the preparatory beat and use a variety of musical styles and dynamic levels. Do not forget that the conductor often needs the warmup period as much as the performers do.

Tuning Procedures

Instrumental ensembles should tune to A-440. A reliable electronic tuner or strobe tuner that is checked periodically against a tuning fork should be used. The practice of tuning higher than A-440 to achieve greater tonal brilliance should definitely be avoided. Mallet percussion are made to play at A-440 and cannot alter their pitch. Wind instruments are also made to play *best in tune* at A-440, 72 degrees farenheit. Any attempt to play noticeably above or below this standard creates severe intonation problems for everyone. (For detailed discussion, read Chapter Three of Kohut's *Instrumental Music Pedagogy*.)

When tuning instrumental ensembles, tune the bass instruments first. This includes string basses, tubas, and low reeds—those instruments that play the roots of the chords in full ensemble. Once the bass instruments are in tune, tune all of the other players to them. The reason for this approach is that good intonation in ensemble performance is achieved by listening and tuning to the roots of the chords, not the upper voices. Tuning the bass instruments first reminds these players that they have the major responsibility for good ensemble intonation. It also immediately focuses the aural attention of the upper voices down to the bottom voices where it should be. Good ensemble intonation is built from the bottom up, not from the top downward. (For detailed information on this topic, see Francis McBeth's *Effective Performance of Band Music*, published by Southern Music Company.)

Traditionally, most bands use the solo clarinet to sound a concert B♭ for tuning at the beginning of rehearsal. Orchestras use the principal oboe to sound an A. In line with the tuning philosophy discussed above, however, we recommend that a tuba sound the band tuning note (either a concert F or B♭) and a bassoon sound a low A for the orchestra. Obviously those players chosen to sound the tuning note must be ones whose pitch is reliable. This means they need to check their pitch frequently against a tuning fork, an electronic tuner, or strobe tuner. When players are given this responsibility, it usually means that they instinctively try harder to play as best in tune as they possibly can.

The tuning done at the very beginning of an instrumental rehearsal should be considered "coarse tuning." Until the instruments and players are fully warmed up, the pitch will fluctuate, usually from flat to sharp. Therefore, "fine tuning" should be delayed until after the ensemble warmup period is finished. All of the bass instruments should be tuned carefully first, the tenors next, then the altos, and finally the sopranos. Good intonation is achieved by tuning from the bottom upward.

THE REHEARSAL PROPER

In preparing for the rehearsal proper the conductor first needs to decide which pieces or sections of pieces are to be rehearsed. Next, establish exactly what is to be accomplished in rehearsing each of the works and how to go about doing it. The following subsections provide guidelines for helping the conductor meet these objectives.

A Basic Outline

The first work scheduled should continue and build on the flow of energy established in the warmup and tuning period. An up-tempo, energetic piece provides a strong start to a concert and can do the same for a rehearsal. This should be a work that the students have worked on before, or because of its relative ease, will provide them with few problems as they perform it.

The piece which requires the most concentrated effort should be scheduled in the middle of the rehearsal period. By this time the students will be thoroughly warmed up, have their concentration at peak level, and thus will probably do their best playing and singing.

Finishing the rehearsal in a positive manner is equally important. In this instance the work need not be of the same style as the opener but should provide the opportunity to complete the rehearsal with a sense of accomplishment and closure. The performers can leave feeling good about themselves and the group, and anxious to come back for more.

In addition to the psychological effect of the rehearsal sequence, keep in mind the musical and physical demands placed on the performers by the pieces that are scheduled. Avoid placing works in consecutive order which put the performers in the extremes of their ranges for long periods. Vary the style and tempo of compositions to be rehearsed. No one enjoys working through an entire rehearsal on slow, legato pieces. Design the rehearsal sequence with the same care that a concert program is designed: the interest of the group should be piqued, built, and brought to a climax.

The preceding basic outline (opener, concentrated effort on more difficult pieces, and closer) may leave the reader with the impression that the opener and closer are merely to be run through and not worked in detail. This is not true. These works should be treated with as much care and rehearsed with as much attention to detail and expression as any other works. A piece scheduled in one of these positions is simply one that has been done in rehearsal for a longer period, has had difficult passages drilled, and now is ready for polishing, and a run-through for continuity.

Synthesis-Analysis-Synthesis

Rehearsal procedure is most effective when it is based on knowledge of learning theory. One of the fundamental theories of music learning is the *synthesis-analysis-synthesis* approach. In this approach, the work or major section to be rehearsed should be introduced in as complete a form as possible. The performers then can gain a sense of the whole piece, or at least an entire section, before working on its individual parts. This "sense of the whole" may be gained by sightreading the piece. In some instances the students' reading skills may not be sufficient to accomplish this, so the teacher may want to use a recording to demonstrate how the piece will eventually sound. Another possibility is for the teacher to play through the composition on the piano. This is easily done in the case of a choral work with relatively few parts and no transposition involved. With a choral work, the teacher also might prepare a small ensemble of advanced students to sing a portion of the piece to demonstrate how it will sound.

After this initial introduction to the work, it should be broken down into its constituent parts and rehearsed in detail. Thorough score study will reveal the sections that will need the greatest amount of rehearsal time and concentrated effort. As specific musical and technical problems arise, each must be attended to and worked back into the context of the piece. When sufficient time has been spent working on the details of the various sections (analysis), the whole work should be reassembled. Thus the cycle is completed by reestablishing the work as a whole.

Even experienced conductors fall into the habit of spending so much time in detailed rehearsals of small sections that the performers seldom, if ever, have the opportunity to experience the work as a whole. Performances following this sort of "parts only" rehearsing tend to be sectionalized, and lacking in a clear vision of how smaller compositional units fit together to create an integrated sense of the complete musical work. Long-range rehearsal planning should, therefore, include sufficient time to run each work without interruption several times to establish the continuity and flow of the music.

Another problem arises when a piece is rehearsed by structural sections—"Let's take it from letter C to letter D again"—without enough attention to the transitional material that connects the sections. These transitional sections often include shifts in tempo, modulatory material, and changes in musical character. The conductor must work on these passages thoroughly and take the time to weave the transitions into the fabric of the piece so that the "seams don't show."

Rehearsal Priorities

There is much to listen for, respond to, correct, and adjust. For young conductors especially, the task can be overwhelming. Even the best prepared students have difficulty knowing what to fix first and what to leave until later. The following is a suggested list of rehearsal priorities. Please view this list as a set of guidelines, not as a rigid formula. Correct pitches and rhythms must precede phrasing and musicality, but that does not mean that early attempts at performing a piece should omit all sense of expression or musicianship. Use these priorities as a mental checklist in your early rehearsal attempts.

1. Correct rhythms and pitches
2. Intonation and tone quality
3. Articulation, bowing, and diction
4. Precision
5. Phrasing and expression
6. Dynamic contrast
7. Balance and blend

CORRECT RHYTHMS AND PITCHES.   The reader will note that rhythm and pitch are listed together as a single rehearsal priority. The reason for this is that, when dealing with both choral and instrumental ensembles, it is impractical to treat rhythm first and pitch second or vice versa. Rhythm is a major concern for instrumentalists because the rhythmic demands in instrumental works are considerably greater than they are in choral compositions. Conversely, pitch is the prime challenge faced by singers who have no fingerings, frets, keyboard, or other tangible aids to help them produce the correct pitch. Despite these differences, the goal for both choral and instrumental ensembles is the same—performing the right notes. This means producing the correct pitches at the proper time.

During initial attempts at a new work, do not try to fix too many things all at once. Instead, apply the principle of "divide and conquer." For example, if there are difficult rhythms to read, having the ensemble perform both the pitches and the rhythms together only complicates matters. Instead have the performers count and intone (or clap or tap) the difficult passage at a slower tempo without pitch. With choral groups, the text of the piece is a further complication. Try difficult intervals without rhythm and on a neutral syllable, then add the correct words and rhythm. These are techniques we have all experienced as performers, but when young conductors are first faced with the problem, the simplest solutions often seem to be the most difficult to recall.

INTONATION AND TONE QUALITY.   Achieving good intonation and performing with pleasing tone quality cannot be accomplished during the rehearsal of a single work. These are established in an on-going, never-ending process of listening and adjustment by both the conductor and the members of the ensemble. The foundation for attaining these goals can be laid in the warmup/teaching period at the beginning of rehearsal and in the training groups which precede top-level performance groups. Yet, even with strong foundations such as these, the development of good tone quality, *appropriate to the work being performed,* and good intonation is a constant challenge to ensembles at all levels.

The key to good intonation as well as good tone quality in singing and wind playing is good tone production. The primary bases of good tone production are breathing and the size and shape of the oral cavity. (For a comprehensive discussion of this topic applicable to both singers and wind players, see Kohut's *Musical Performance,* Part III.)

ARTICULATION, BOWING, AND DICTION.   Articulation, bowing, and diction are the processes through which the musical material is specifically delineated and more clearly defined. Phrase structure is made comprehensible by these processes. In instrumental music, specific pitches and note groups are emphasized by appropriate articulations and bowings, while in choral music, good diction carries the meaning of the text to the listener. A strong argument can be made that diction, in particular the purity and unification of vowel sounds, is inseparable from the production of good tone quality in singing. We have chosen to list diction with articulation and bowing as a matter of rehearsal procedure, not as an argument for separating vowel production and color from tone quality.

PRECISION.   Precision is formally defined as the degree of refinement with which an operation is performed. Musical precision has to do with specific events occurring in time and whether the ensemble members execute those events simultaneously. Stated simply, "Are we all doing the same thing at the same time?" Attacks, releases, entrances of separate sections, variations in tempo (ritardando and accelerando), and especially the execution of rhythms, are all affected by the degree of precision achieved by the ensemble. The primary arbiter of this degree of precision is the conductor.

PHRASING AND EXPRESSION.   Performing with musicality and expression is not accomplished in the final stages of rehearsal only. It should not be like icing on a cake, but should be encouraged as a continual part of the music making and rehearsal process.

Student conductors will discover, however, that asking for expressive playing and singing too early in the rehearsal procedure may be self-defeating. Trying to perform a musical line expressively while incorrect pitches and rhythms are present only makes the learning process more difficult. We must walk before we run; thus it is usually wise to establish the basics before moving on to more complex matters.

DYNAMIC CONTRAST. An integral part of phrase shaping and expression is dynamic contrast and nuance. Sections of a work which have broadly contrasting dynamic levels certainly should be emphasized in early rehearsals. Areas requiring more subtle shadings can be saved until more fundamental matters have been addressed.

BALANCE AND BLEND. Balance involves loudness and whether or not individual performers or whole sections are too loud or too soft in relation to the rest of the ensemble. Blend is the degree to which a homogeneous sound is achieved among the members of a section and among all sections of the ensemble combined. The conductor is in the best position to listen for and guide the ensemble in attaining good balance and a well-blended sound. At the same time, the performers themselves must be trained to accept a major role in listening and cooperating to achieve good balance and blend.

Error Detection and Correction

When the conductor really knows the score, error detection is usually a relatively easy, routine matter. Difficulties arise when the conductor does not know the score well and tries to "read" while conducting. The mind is simply overwhelmed as it tries to sort and categorize the visual information from the score and the aural information from the ensemble simultaneously.

Early efforts in rehearsal should focus on detection and correction of simple musical errors, i.e., discrepancies between what the conductor knows of the score and what is in fact being performed. Incorrect pitches and rhythms within a passage should be pointed out and suggestions for improvement made. To help systematize your thinking and correct the mistakes, we suggest the following three types of responses which are most frequently used by experienced conductors:

1. *Direct verbal instruction.* In this response mode little explanation is needed. The error is identified and the solution provided. "Clarinets, in measure 24 you played B♭. It should be B♮." "Altos, please sing softer in this section."

2. *Conductor modeling.* Because music is a nonverbal form of expression, some corrections cannot be effectively accomplished with words and verbal explanations. Describing how a phrase should be shaped or what the proper tone quality should be is inevitably less effective than having the performers *hear* how it should sound. The conductor should sing the

musical phrase or tone desired and then have the performers sing it back.

When you model via singing, it is important (especially when working with choral groups) that your voice represents a very high quality model in all aspects of the performance. You may be attempting to correct a specific pitch or rhythm only, but in doing so, constant subliminal information about technique (posture, breathing, tone quality), pronunciation, and musicality also is being provided. The object of the demonstration may be simple note correction, but if performed with a good quality tone and expressive phrase shape, the performers will soon realize that these things are expected of them on a consistent basis as well.

3. *Descriptive language or psychological images.* In some instances verbal descriptors or the use of psychological imaging can be an effective means of eliciting the desired musical response from the performers. "You don't have the melody sopranos. Just let your line float above the other voices." "Trumpets, the fanfare passage should sound like the gates of heaven opening." Unfortunately, this type of response is often the most frequently used and sometimes the least effective. It should be used judiciously and, for best results, coupled with teacher modeling.

It is extremely important when using any of the response modes that the performers try out the conductor's suggestion immediately. This is obvious to an experienced conductor, but student conductors too frequently fall into the unproductive habit of only identifying the problem without providing a solution. "That's not quite right, let's try it again," provides no useful information to young performers and often is equally worthless for more advanced performers. Instead, the *specific* rhythm, interval, dynamic level, or articulation must be isolated, demonstrated, and practiced by the performers, then reintegrated into the larger phrase before real improvement can be realized.

An analogy that is helpful in better understanding this problem can be made with the role and function of the physician. When we are ill, the physician listens to our description of what is wrong, examines us for the symptoms, compares what he sees with what is known of the many illnesses, and makes a diagnosis. The physician then prescribes a medication or gives instructions to be followed to cure the illness. It is not an infallible procedure, but it is the most effective one that we know. Conductors should operate in the same fashion: listening to the ensemble perform, noting the mistakes and areas that need improvement, and *providing solutions.* It is in the last step where many conductors are inefficient. Problems are identified but no solutions are provided.

After much experience in rehearsal situations the conductor also needs to be aware of, and begin to listen for, mistakes in performance technique as well as purely musical errors. In many instances under-developed or inadequate performance skill is the underlying cause of musical problems. If the singer or wind player cannot adequately sustain a musical line with proper breath support, intonation will suffer. If the performers' technique is not flexible and agile, intricate rhythms cannot be performed accurately. The conductor must possess the skill and knowledge to identify and correct such problems. (See the Bibliography for books that provide solutions for these specific kinds of problems.)

Pacing

While developing skills in error detection and correction, young conductors also need to develop a feel for the pace at which the rehearsal moves. Technically speaking, pace can be defined as the speed at which one moves from one activity to another in the rehearsal, yet it involves much more than that. A key ingredient in the mix of activities that constitutes rehearsal pacing is the personal energy, enthusiasm, musicality, and intensity displayed by the conductor. In most circumstances, the performers will directly reflect those same qualities in their rehearsal responses. Confidence also is instilled in the group if its members perceive in the conductor a secure knowledge of the music, a genuine enthusiasm for the piece being rehearsed, and a willingness to work constructively with the members of the ensemble.

Another important factor in pacing is balancing the amount of talk (instructions, directions, fielding questions, and responding) with the amount of singing or playing. Early ventures by the young conductor invariably contain too much talk and too little performing. Too much time is also spent trying to explain what is desired rather than indicating it with the conducting gesture or demonstrating it vocally. When and if the young conductor finally gets around to demonstrating what is to be changed, the usual tendency is to move on to new material without any follow-up drill on the former. The assumption made is that the verbal instructions and demonstration are sufficient to solve the problem. They seldom are.

It cannot be emphasized too strongly that teaching and learning are separate activities. Until the performers *themselves* have tried and demonstrated the new technique or corrected the mistake *in fact,* the conductor should not assume that the passage will be any better the next time the group attempts it. In other words, the performers must not only understand what the conductor wants, they must also be able to execute it. This requires trying it out at least once. Sometimes it requires several rehearsal trials.

Avoiding Excessive Verbosity

One of the quickest ways to bore an ensemble and put the performers to sleep is with excessive talk and verbal explanation. This is especially true when the conductor gives numerous preliminary instructions before giving the downbeat for a new piece to be read for the first time. One or two brief comments are usually sufficient in this situation. Sometimes no comments are in order. Just tell the ensemble the name of the piece and give the downbeat; do not waste time talking about things that will not be remembered by anyone anyway. After playing or singing through the piece once, verbal comments may then for the first time have some value and relevance.

When doing detailed rehearsal analysis, work on one problem at a time. Limit your verbal directions to one or two concise statements. Most often, vocal modeling will be the most efficient method for solving the problem. The performers should then try the specific spot in question, and finally, reintegrate it into the larger phrase or passage.

Avoid discussing several different problems in summary form with no rehearsal drill in between. The performers, especially inexperienced ones, will not be able to remember and execute four or five corrections at once. Even when the instructions are brief, the conductor needs to be sure that the group is genuinely attentive. Otherwise, all time and effort are wasted.

In summary, avoid excessive talking and verbal description and analysis in rehearsal. Music is a nonverbal form of artistic expression. In rehearsal, particularly when dealing with phrasing, style, and expression, *sing* what you want. Not only is it much more effective than verbal description, it also takes far less time.

Sectional and Individual Problems

A good, efficient rehearsal is one where primary emphasis is on full ensemble problems with correspondingly less emphasis on sectional and individual problems. If a large number of purely sectional and individual problems need attention, then outside sectional rehearsals and individual conferences should be scheduled. Do not try to solve sectional and individual problems in the full rehearsal with a majority of the ensemble resting and doing nothing most of the time. At the very least, this inexcusable waste of people's time will result in boredom. At worst, in a school situation, it can bring about severe discipline problems. Full ensemble rehearsals should focus mainly on full ensemble problems.

The above does not mean that sectional and individual problems should not be dealt with at all in full rehearsal. A limited amount of time spent in rehearsing sections and individuals is both proper and prudent. After this is done, however, reintegrate the full ensemble by having it join the section or individual in the final run-through of the rehearsed passage. In this way, the full ensemble still gets to be involved even though the rehearsal drill itself was directed toward only a small segment of the whole.

If the teacher/conductor is continually faced with the need for lots of sectional and individual rehearsal, this probably indicates that the music being used is too difficult. Every good ensemble deserves to be challenged somewhat, but there are limits to how much challenge is wise. Music that is too difficult usually results in rehearsal time spent mainly in "chasing notes." (One might as well forget about musical expression, because there will not be sufficient time to get to that.) Such rehearsals dominated by rote drill get boring in a hurry. They also tend to bring on feelings of futility and frustration. The solution in this case is for the conductor to do a better job of prerehearsal planning, especially in the selection of music for the ensemble.

Drilling Difficult Passages

When a difficult rhythmic or technical passage is encountered in rehearsal, the traditional prescription is to isolate that passage and drill it once or twice at a much slower tempo and then take it back up to tempo. This seems so obvious, yet young conductors in their first rehearsal attempts often forget to do this. Instead they drill the passage up to tempo and are then puzzled as to why it does not improve. This is one reason why taping all of one's rehearsals is so valuable. If the conductor cannot figure out during the rehearsal why a given technique is not working, then he or she has a much better chance of figuring it out later when reviewing the tape.

Slowing down the tempo is the first and most obvious thing to do in trying to work out a difficult passage. If this does not quickly solve the problem, then the conductor needs to divide the musical elements and conquer them one at a time. For example, if rhythm is the main source of difficulty, deal with it alone by counting aloud and clapping the patterns if necessary. Perhaps all that is needed is simply to sing or play the patterns on a single repeated pitch until they can be executed accurately. Then add the written pitches. If difficult melodic writing is present, isolate the specific intervals in question and work on each one separately. This may be done by playing or singing through the related scale and "filling in" the scale tones within the wide interval. (On a more general level, the consistent use of a pitch reading method like solfege or numbers will help immensely with pitch location.) Other problems such as rapid changes in dynamics or style and use of frequent off-beat accents should be handled in similar fashion. Neutralize the pitch and other musical factors so that you can focus on the problem area alone.

In choral music, a special challenge is presented by the combination of musical elements with a text. Solve the musical problems by singing on a neutral syllable, then add the text. In the case of a foreign language, the conductor must be able to model the pronunciations and then provide practice for the singers. Speaking the language to the written rhythmic values before attempting the pitches can also help greatly in some cases.

The final step in this process is to reintegrate all of the parts back into the whole—reassemble the "nuts and bolts" of melody, rhythm, tempo, harmony, pronunciation, and dynamics into the larger context of the work. This may mean adding one element at a time, such as performing well-tuned harmonies chord by chord, then doing them slowly with written note values, and finally singing up to tempo. As another example, begin by speaking the text in rhythm only, then rhythm and pitch only on a neutral syllable, and finally, rhythm, pitch, and text in combination. In all cases the final step of reintegration is critical. Without it, the individual learnings will remain unconnected and ineffective, and thus represent rehearsal time and effort that was largely wasted.

Miscellaneous Problems

1. "Tenors, your pitch is flat," or "Clarinets, play that more staccato." When the conductor gives general instructions like these, it is all too easy for the individuals to assume that someone else in the section is at fault and make no adjustment. Listen to that problem section again very carefully to be certain that a real change in sound has occurred. Do not assume that because you have said it, it will necessarily happen. Make the performers prove their understanding and ability to do what you want via performance playback.

2. If, for example, you hear wrong notes and cannot figure out who is doing it, listen to the ensemble section by section, slowly, until you locate the problem. In extreme cases you may find it necessary to hear individual performers alone, but be very careful not to get "bogged down" doing this while the rest of the ensemble sits and waits for you to finish.

3. Explaining where to start within the body of a piece is sometimes a source of confusion caused by inexperienced rehearsal directors. Saying "start eight measures before letter A" and giving a downbeat soon afterward inevitably means that most of the performers will not have had enough time to locate the right spot. To avoid this type of problem, get in the habit of saying, "Before letter A, count back with me: 1, 2, 3, 4, 5, 6, 7, 8. Begin on the eighth measure before letter A."

   With choral music, in which all parts are printed and each page contains several staves or "systems," state the starting place beginning with the page, then the system, measure, and finally the beat. Using the text as a guide may be effective, but only if all parts have the same text to the same rhythm; otherwise it will only complicate things.

4. Most musicians have seen orchestral conductors vibrate the left hand in simulation of a violin vibrato when they want more vibrato and intensity from a given string section. We would like to recommend two other visual cues of equivalent value. One is to tug on the left ear lobe with the thumb and index finger of the left hand to indicate that more careful listening is needed because the intonation is poor. Another cue specifically for singers and wind players is to place the left hand middle finger against your abdomen and vibrate as if you were a cellist. This cue says "more and better breath support, please; your tones are sagging and the pitch is going flat." All of these can be real savers of rehearsal time since you can communicate what the problem is without having to stop the group.

5. When obvious wrong notes are performed, do not stop the ensemble. It wastes time and only adds to the frustration already felt by the guilty performer. Such wrong notes usually solve themselves during the next run-through. The obvious exception is with young musicians who are unaware that they just produced a wrong pitch or inaccurate rhythm. They need to be told and assisted with the corrections.

6. Do not stop the ensemble if you have nothing to say. Have a good reason for stopping and explain it clearly to the group.

7. Work toward development of a wide dynamic range. Avoid performing at mezzoforte all of the time.

8. Do not be afraid to use rubato in appropriate places. Judicious use of rubato is an integral part of musical expression. At the same time, do

not overdo its use. Avoid overconducting in all of its forms. Strive to make all of your gestures clear and functional. Leave flowery, excessive movements to the "showmen."

REHEARSAL TEACHING AND EVALUATION

As stated earlier, the conductor of school ensembles must be prepared to teach the fundamentals of musicianship and performance technique, as well as conduct and rehearse. The most fundamental skill to be taught is music reading. Other basic rehearsal and performance techniques to be learned by student musicians include watching the conductor, ensemble listening, intonation, and maintaining steady tempi. Finally, teacher/conductors must also be prepared to evaluate their ensembles and the effectiveness of their own teaching. These are the topics covered in this section.

Music Reading

Being able to read music is essential to good ensemble performance. To most instrumentalists this is obvious. They are expected to learn how to read fairly soon after starting an instrument and spend hours of home practice improving their reading skill, as well as performance technique. With singers, this is not the case. Most young singers are not taught to read music; they learn the pieces they sing by rote. The teacher sings through the song, phrase by phrase, and the students sing it back repeatedly until the song is learned. This is the appropriate method for teaching very young singers new pieces. At the same time, the music teacher may be having the students learn note values, the names of the lines and spaces of the staff, definitions of expressive terms, and so on. This too is appropriate learning for young singers. Unfortunately, learning in these two areas (learning pieces for enjoyment and performance, and learning theoretical knowledge and skills) is seldom combined in a sequence of instruction that produces desirable outcomes. The exclusive use of rote teaching too frequently continues through middle and high school with only lip service paid to the development of genuine music reading skills. The result is one of musical illiteracy—the singers cannot read!

To counter this problem, the teacher/conductor must establish a systematic method of *thinking about and teaching* music reading skills. Merely passing out a new piece and stumbling through it on a neutral syllable, with or without the piano, will not suffice. Instead, establish relationships in sound first. This can be done by singing melodic exercises to solfege syllables or scale step numbers to establish the intervallic relationships in the singers' ears and minds. If solfege is used, simple diatonic and triadic patterns allow the singers to become accustomed to singing the syllables in the proper order without having to think about them. By using solfege patterns as warmup exercises early in the year, the syllables will be quickly ingrained and easy to work with.

While the singers are becoming familiar with solfege patterns, they should also be trained to use "inner hearing," that is, to think the pitch before it is sung. This same technique of hearing the pitch in the mind's ear allows a singer to memorize and recall the tonal center and pitch level of a composition while it is being sung. Tonal memory is an important skill for the choral singer and can be developed through exercises and in-class activities.

Once the relationships of sound and syllable have been established in the singers' ears and minds, relationships between symbols and sound can be established. An early method for this may be using the Curwen hand signs as used in the Kodàly method. This can soon lead to the use of written syllable names (*do, re, mi,* etc.) or the initial letter of the syllable. Eventually standard notation is substituted for these icons and genuine music reading can commence.

The final step in this process is to transfer these learnings into the regular rehearsal setting. They must be applied to real music to be of value, and the teacher/conductor needs a workable plan for achieving this. For example, as each piece is started, have the singers: (1) identify the key center (find *do*), (2) sing through the tonic triad, (3) visually locate *do* in their voice parts, (4) determine the syllable or scale step on which their parts begin, and (5) engage their brains and tonal memories so that they can always inwardly hear and maintain the tonal center.

Learning to read music is not a simple task. Like good intonation and other fundamentals, it takes considerable time and effort to master. The best solution is to start as soon as possible, use a method that is known to work well, and be persistent in your efforts to achieve success.

The ultimate goal of learning to read music is to become a fluent sightreader. To achieve this goal, do the following:

1. Get a book designed specifically for rhythmic drill and master all of the patterns. An alternate approach is simply to get a snare drum method book and use it for rhythmic drill purposes.

2. Get a good sightsinging book and practice until you can sing all of the tunes and exercises in it at sight. Instrumentalists in particular should also work concurrently on scales, arpeggios, and scales in thirds. This further aids development of the ear in terms of tonality and pitch, in addition to improving general performance technique.

3. Last and most important is to do *lots* of sightreading within the ensemble's level of difficulty. Performing duets, trios, and other small combinations is also highly recommended. The more actual sightreading experience you have, the better sightreader you will be.

Intonation

Fundamental to the development of high quality performance at any level is the ability to sing or play with correct intonation. This discussion will focus mainly on intonation in the choral setting. A detailed discussion of intonation as it relates to instrumental performance is found in Chapter Three of Kohut's *Instrumental Music Pedagogy.*

Many factors affect the pitch and intonation of ensemble singing. For purposes of discussion they can be separated into the areas of (1) aural and vocal skills, (2) musical concepts, and (3) psychological approaches. For practical training on a daily basis to be effective, however, work in these three areas must be integrated. This training should be initiated during the warmup or teaching period preceding the actual rehearsal. This is so that the singers can concentrate on the development of these skills without the distraction of following the score, singing a part, or making music. Yet this training is ineffective unless it is constantly reinforced and woven directly into the fabric of the rehearsal and the music making process.

AURAL AND VOCAL SKILLS. In simplest terms, to reproduce any pitch, the singer must do three things: listen, think, and sing. Whether the pitch is sounded by an external source or is simply picked from within, the process must begin with a clear concept of the pitch to be reproduced. The singer first hears and "thinks" the pitch, adjusts the vocal mechanism to sound the tone which has been perceived, and finally begins the act of singing, as breath is added to the appropriately stretched vocal folds. As the new vocal tone is produced, the cycle begins again. The singer now listens to the pitch currently being sung, makes incremental adjustments as needed, and begins to locate and create a mental aural image of the next pitch of the phrase.

Inexperienced singers sometimes reverse or short-circuit this process. Singing begins in the general location of the desired pitch and *then* listening and adjustment may (or may not) occur. The result is one of "scooping" or sliding into pitches, with the result that intonation generally is inaccurate. If the correct process of *listen-think-sing* is instilled in even the youngest singers, they will have a much better chance of producing well-tuned pitches.

Accurate pitch reproduction and intonation is based largely on active, intelligent listening. The ensemble members should be encouraged to use omnidirectional listening; they must be taught *what* to listen for, as well. The general instruction, "Listen!" has little effect on inexperienced performers. They simply do not know what to listen for. First, they must be taught to listen carefully to their own voices, then to others in their section, and eventually to intonation among the other sections as well. In addition to this normal kind of external listening, singers must also develop a keen sense of inner hearing or audiation. It is the development of this pitch memory which enables the singer to lock a tonal center into the mind and ear, and maintain it throughout a work. Without it, flatting or sharping may occur during a piece even though the tuning of individual chords is good.

Equally important to the development of coordination between ear and voice is the proper use of the vocal instrument itself. A buoyant, dynamic posture must be established to allow the voice to function in its most natural, vibrant manner. The breath is perhaps the single most important factor in the singing process and is directly dependent on good posture. Without a well-managed supply of air, the voice cannot function effectively and correct pitch cannot be maintained.

The vocal resonators, particularly the primary areas of the mouth and throat, must be open and free to play their part in the production of quality tone and accurate pitch making. Even with correct posture and adequate breath support, a closed mouth, tight jaw, or constricted throat will produce a dull, flaccid tone and correspondingly poor pitch. Opening the mouth and throat to create the feeling of vertical, inward space is the key to a well-tuned, fully resonant sound.

The production of pure, unified vowels is also a factor in accurate pitch production. Poorly matched vowels within or between sections can create the impression of out-of-tune singing, even when intonation is perfect. A similar effect can occur if the vibrato of individual singers is so unruly that it disturbs the ensemble sound. In both cases (vowels and vibrato) the solution is one of teaching the singers to listen and cooperate with their voices, rather than compete with them.

MUSICAL CONCEPTS.   In addition to the development of aural and vocal skills, student performers must gain a knowledge of the musical and expressive concepts that pertain to intonation and well-tuned singing. First, provide the singers with a clear understanding of what it means to make small changes in pitch and provide experiences in doing so. Young singers not only lack coordination in pitch making; they also do not have appropriate terms attached to the skills they do have. This can be heard as a section struggles to "get the pitch up!" but actually only succeeds in having its members sing louder, use a brighter vowel, shove the chin farther out of line, and generally push the vocal tone to its limits. To avoid this situation, singers should have experiences with, and proper terms for, incremental changes in loudness, vowel color, tone production, and pitch.

Dynamics can also affect singers' ability to sing well in tune. Oversinging and forcing the tone in an attempt to perform loud dynamic levels can cause sharping. Softer singing allows for better listening and generally better intonation. However, soft singing does carry with it the risk of being lazy and unenergetic, and therefore sounding "under pitch."

Slowing the tempo to accommodate pitch location and the reading of rhythms as a new work is introduced is common practice. Intonation in difficult spots may improve if each chord is held beyond its written length so that more thorough listening can take place. To increase the speed at which the singers can employ the listen-think-sing process, rehearse at or near performance tempo but in full staccato style. This increases the "think" time but eliminates any time to adjust the pitch after it is sounded. Thus, each interval and chord must be heard, thought, and tuned in the mind *before* it is sung.

A strong sense of rhythmic drive can also help prevent sagging pitch. Without the inner propulsion of rhythmic subdivision, the unit beat, although steady, can become dull and passive. The physical involvement of tapping or clapping the subdivision can be of great benefit to feeling the movement of line and pitch. Seldom do we have pitch problems in pieces with a quick tempo and active rhythms. It is the slow, sustained pieces that deserve our "subdivided" attention.

PSYCHOLOGICAL APPROACHES.   The phrase "psychological approaches" is employed here to denote the use of mental imagery, verbal description, and metaphoric language to elicit changes in physical actions. Unfortunately, such devices are often the most frequently used but the least successful means of improving poor pitch and faulty intonation. Particularly ineffective is the use of disconnected verbal directions, phrases that may mean something to the conductor but which have no meaning to the performers. We have all experienced directions like, "float the pitch up," "lift those tones," "raise your eyebrows," and the ultimate in meaningless instruction, "think higher." Phrases such as these are ineffective if used in isolation and "disconnected" from experience. Unless the singers have actually *experienced* changing pitch or improving intonation and connected it with floating, lifting, raising, or thinking, such terms will remain meaningless and without value.

OTHER FACTORS AFFECTING INTONATION.   General physical and psychological conditions may also contribute to chronic flatting and inaccurate intonation. Matters as simple as poor ventilation, weather conditions, or room acoustics, and as complex as physical and mental fatigue, anxiety, and boredom have a telling effect on pitch production and tuning.

Teaching the Ensemble to Watch

An essential part of being a good ensemble member is learning to watch the conductor. The conductor's job is to help the ensemble members learn this skill. The first steps were given in Chapter 1 where we detailed the importance of the conductor: (1) looking directly at the ensemble to get their attention and eye contact, (2) assuming an authoritative stance and "ready position," (3) counting one measure silently, and (4) executing a confident preparatory-downbeat sequence while simultaneously breathing with the ensemble. If the conductor is doing all of these things and the attacks are still sloppy and insecure, he or she should watch and listen to the ensemble very carefully to determine the cause. They may not be coming to a full "ready position" with the conductor. They may be breathing too soon or too late. Whatever the problem, the conductor must be insistent and persistent in efforts to achieve consistently good attacks. The performers need to be reminded that they must really "see" (concentrate) when they look at the conductor. Merely aiming one's eyes toward the conductor is not enough.

Poor attacks are not always caused by inattentive ensemble members. Sometimes conductors inadvertently teach their groups *not to watch.* One of the worst things one can do in this regard is to give them a verbal countdown (one, two, ready, begin) for the first attack. Almost as bad is to habitually count *and conduct* a couple of extra beats (three, four, begin) before each attack while rehearsing. Both of these bad habits should be scrupulously avoided. Instead, establish good eye contact with the ensemble, assume a firm ready position, and give a clean, clear, and solid downbeat.

Another form of what we call verbal conducting is to give verbal instructions *while* the ensemble is performing: ''softer, sssshhhh''; ''watch for the accent coming up.'' And then there are those who bang the baton on the conductor's stand and yell ''one- and two-and three-and four-and'' over the sound of the group. All of these, especially the latter, literally insure that the performers learn to glue their eyes to the page and never look up. Why should they look up? Probably nothing of any real value can be gleaned from the conductor's hand gestures; the only concrete information provided exists in the form of verbal instructions. The message then is very clear: don't bother *watching;* just *listen* to the conductor.

The novice conductor often adds to this problem by not maintaining good eye contact with the performers. Why should they watch the conductor whose head is in the score? Maximize the effectiveness of your conducting by *visually showing* your ensemble what you want rather than by *verbally telling* them.

In Chapter 1 we also discussed the problem of performers rushing and dragging the tempo, and the following solutions were given: (1) When the ensemble rushes, slow down the tempo and increase your beat size as in ritard. (2) When the ensemble drags, speed up your tempo and decrease your beat size as in an accelerando. Usually these approaches solve the respective problems. If not, try the following: Have the performers follow your beat patterns and count aloud (no singing or playing) while you conduct. Begin with a four pattern and vary the tempo faster and slower. Then do the same with a three pattern and with a two pattern. Finally, mix the patterns while continuing to vary the tempo. The goal is to get them to watch each and every beat very carefully.

As a corollary to the above, vary not only the tempo but also the style, articulation, and dynamics, and have the group respond in kind with their counting. As the performers become more familiar with the piece where the tempo problems first occurred, the same procedures can be used with the music to reinforce the importance of careful watching.

Carefully watching the conductor's beat will not in itself bring about superior ensemble precision. Each performer still must learn to *listen* to the other performers as well as *watch* the conductor. This is especially true when performing in an unfamiliar auditorium or concert hall. When performing in a very large rehearsal room or concert stage where the physical distance between performers is great, careful listening is absolutely essential. In all cases, good precision is only the first step. Performing with good ensemble intonation, balance, and blend, plus homogeneity of musical expression also requires careful listening. Teaching ensemble performers the importance of careful listening is the purpose of the next subsection.

Teaching Ensemble Listening

Good ensemble intonation, balance, blend, and precision are vital to quality performance. The responsibility for achieving these factors belongs equally to the performers and the conductor. The conductor may be in the best position to listen to the overall effect of the ensemble and its various sections, but only the performers themselves can make the changes needed—through careful listening and adjustment. This sense of individual responsibility should be stressed continually by the conductor.

Another important factor is ensemble tone quality. Again the conductor's responsibility is to remind the performers of their individual responsibility in this area. "Listen to the quality of your tone. Is it radically different from those near you? What kind of adjustments can you make so that the sound of your section is more homogeneous in quality?" In making this recommendation, we do not mean to imply that every performer should sacrifice personal technique in order to make her or his voice or instrument sound identical to all others. Reasonable accommodation is all that is required. The goal is to produce a well-blended, homogeneous sound, as dictated by the music being performed. With singers particularly, this sense of tonal blend can be greatly enhanced by using purely formed, unified vowels—produced the same from person to person and section to section throughout the choir.

Tempo Considerations

Establishing the proper tempo for each piece is one of the *most* important tasks of the conductor. For every composition there is a relatively small acceptable range of tempi in which the work will "live and thrive." A composition marked $\quarternote = 120$ can probably be performed acceptably within a range of $\quarternote = 108$–132 but may in fact feel musically "uncomfortable" beyond these limits. Therefore, in the early stages of score study and preparation, experiment with slightly different tempi before locking into a consistent pace. Take the time to note the number of beats per minute that you use in your experimentation. The ability to establish specific metronomic markings can and should be learned, but until it is, check yourself carefully. By studying the music, consulting your conducting teacher, listening to recordings and developing your own musical "sense," the proper tempo can eventually be discovered.

VARYING THE TEMPO FOR LEARNING.   As noted in the section on intonation, a common practice when introducing a new work is to slow down the tempo to facilitate easier pitch and rhythmic reading. This is a logical procedure and can often be helpful, but care should be taken that the tempo is not slowed to such an extreme that it becomes difficult, if not impossible, to get it up to the proper tempo later. The reason for this is that the execution of performance fundamentals like breathing, bowing, and tonguing, for example, changes significantly when going from a very slow to a fast tempo. The corresponding kinesthetic sensations are also quite different. The consequence of working very slowly on a piece for an extended period is that the ensemble learns a piece that is quite different from the same piece performed up to tempo. To put it another way, the teacher, in the final analysis, ends up teaching two pieces. Unfortunately, the version attempted at the proper tempo may never sound quite right.

This problem of practicing too long at a slow tempo is a common pitfall for young conductors. The new piece is difficult for the ensemble. Sightreading the piece at anywhere near the proper tempo is out of the question, so the conductor decides to drill it very slowly. Another possibility is to put that piece away and try it again when your group is capable of performing it. Selecting music that matches the performance capabilities of your ensemble is a skill that comes with experience. Choose music that can be performed up to tempo (or close to it) without excessive "breakdowns." Such music will allow the conductor to spend the bulk of rehearsal time working on intonation, balance, blend, attacks and releases, and musical expression, rather than "chasing notes" and doing rote drill of difficult rhythms and melodic intervals.

BEAT DIVISIONS OR MICRORHYTHMS.   One of the most effective means of accurately maintaining the tempo and of creating the feeling of energetic motion within the musical line is the use of beat divisions or microrhythms. Both the conductor and performers alike can benefit from this practice. Instead of counting and thinking only the unit pulse, they should experience in as many ways possible the smallest practical unit of the beat.

For example, while tapping the unit beat, speak the divisions; clap the sixteenth note subdivisions while singing the written rhythms; perform the written pitches but articulate the micropulse within each longer written value, as shown in Example 29.

Encourage the performers to think and "feel" the micropulses within longer values. Instead of thinking of a half note in common time as two big beats, think of it as, at least, four eighths, and possibly eight sixteenths if the tempo is slow enough. As you conduct, do not allow your

EXAMPLE 29.

rhythmic sense to plod along with the beat pattern. Mentally divide the beats in order to maintain an accurate, energetic tempo.

The Use of Audio and Video Tape for Evaluation

The acts of conducting and rehearsing are evaluative in nature. As was mentioned early in the text, the conductor should be listening constantly and comparing what is known with what is being heard. The continuous loop of performing, listening, evaluating, adjusting, and performing again, is the essence of the conductor's task. It is not an easy one. With the large number of aural "channels of information" bombarding the conductor, it is next to impossible to decipher and process all of it simultaneously.

To make this process easier, more can be learned about what is happening in rehearsal through the use of audio or video tape. By taping segments or entire rehearsals, the conductor can replay and more carefully "decode" all of the signals. In rehearsal, your attention may be focused on one problematic aspect of the sound while other things are going astray as well. By listening to the tape without the pressure of rehearsal pacing, conducting, and so on, you will hear those "other things" you failed to hear during the actual rehearsal.

In the same way that the group's performance can be reanalyzed, conducting and rehearsal techniques also can be more carefully observed on video tape. By video taping rehearsal episodes we can clearly see the conducting gestures used, the amount of talk and performance going on, and most important, the effect that all of these have on the improvement of the ensemble (or the lack of it).

A well-structured observation list or schedule can also greatly help the analysis of these tapes. List the types of rehearsal activities that should be taking place and compare this with what is shown or heard on tape. Count the number of instances of specific conducting/teaching behaviors, or measure the time spent in giving directions, fielding questions, and actually making music. Such comparisons can be extremely useful in planning and carrying out future rehearsals.

CHORAL STANDING ARRANGEMENTS

A significant change in the sound of a choral ensemble can be achieved by moving entire sections into various positions, moving individual singers within each section, or by mixing the singers into quartets. The sound heard by both the singers and the audience will be noticeably different in each of these situations. The primary reasons for varying sectional and individual singer placement, therefore, are aural and stylistic. Balance, blend, and intonation can also be greatly enhanced, depending on the conductor's choice of sectional placement. (For excellent diagrams of instrumental seating arrangements, see Green's *The Modern Conductor*, p. 245ff. and Hunsberger and Ernst's *The Art of Conducting*, p. 331ff.)

DIAGRAM 31

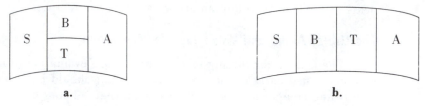

a.   b.

Positioning for Ideal Balance

Several fundamental principles should be noted in determining the placement of sections and individuals. First, the audience will hear best those voices placed in the front and center of the choir. This principle can be applied by placing sections with relatively few singers (notoriously the tenors) or relatively weak singers in the first two rows and in the center of the ensemble, as shown in Diagram 31a. If the sections and the individual voices are relatively equal in number and loudness, the sections can be arranged in columns as shown in Diagram 31b. This allows the audience to hear a balanced presentation from each voice part.

Tuning to the Basses

A second principle is that singers hear best those voices and sections that are closest to them. By placing the sopranos and basses next to each other as shown in Diagram 31b, these parts, which frequently have octaves to tune, will be in closest proximity. Also, the inner parts are also close to each other for easier tuning and balance. Also related to this principle is the fact that performers more readily hear those behind them than those in front or to the sides. For this reason the arrangement in Diagram 32 allows everyone to hear the basses readily and tune to them more easily.

To use the arrangement in Diagram 32, the basses must have relatively strong voices in order to "sing through" the other sections and be heard. They must also be secure, independent musicians as they will not be able to hear the other sections or the other members of their own section as well as in other formations.

DIAGRAM 32

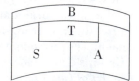

DIAGRAM 33

```
S B T A  S B T A
T A B S  T A B S
B S A T  B S A T
A T S B  A T S B
```

Mixed Quartets

Many conductors place their singers in mixed quartets throughout the choir for the best results in balance, blend, and tuning (see Diagram 33). In this setting each singer has at least one singer from each of the other sections nearby with whom to tune and balance. Even so, each singer should still be encouraged to listen to other singers in all directions, not just the quartet in his or her row. Musically, the ensemble still has to function as a unified choir.

The success of the preceding formation also is dependent on the choir members being relatively equal in number and independent as musicians. In younger choirs where weaker singers and weaker readers depend heavily on stronger section members for support, such an arrangement may be impractical. This situation can be improved, however, by simply having the music learned thoroughly in sectional formation before moving to the scrambled arrangement.

The style of the music being performed should also be taken into consideration before assigning sectional positions. In an ideal setting, the mixed quartet formation lends itself best to tuning, balance, and blend with homophonic music where a homogeneous sound is desirable. On the other hand, polyphonic music is best served by sectional arrangements since a strong sense of part independence and aural clarity are important in this type of music.

Placement of Individuals Within a Section

In the same way that the sound of an ensemble can be changed by the position of the sections in the group, so can the sound of the sections be altered by the placement of the individual singers within the rows of the section. The factors with which the conductor must be concerned are the size and quality of each voice and the reading and musicianship skills of each singer.

There is a wide range of opinion regarding the placement of individuals within the section. Some conductors choose to assign seats by height without regard for the sound of the voices. Many conductors use the procedures espoused by Weston Noble at Luther College to match voices within the section to help achieve better balance, blend, and intonation. In this process each singer in the section sings a familiar song *(My Country 'Tis of Thee)* with every other member of the section. The conductor

DIAGRAM 34

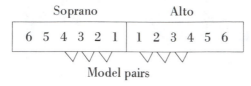

Model pairs

listens to the various matches and by repeating this process with various pairs, eventually arrives at a pair of singers that sound the best, and feel most comfortable singing together.

It is important to note that this "model pair" consists of the two individuals that *sound best together,* not the two that sound most alike. These singers are placed in the center of the choir (Position 1 and 2 in Diagram 34). The procedure is then repeated until a third singer is paired with singer 2, then 3 with 4, 4 with 5, and so on. This must be done for each row of the choir, and for all sections.

During the procedure the singers should be encouraged to use their own natural singing voice and not try to imitate or "match" the voice of the singer with whom they are singing. The model pairs should occur naturally and not be forced by changing quality or natural resonance.

With young or undeveloped voices, the matching procedure described is accomplished with relative ease because the voices within the section are very similar. Individual vocal characteristics of color and vibrato are undeveloped and many of the voices will sound alike. With more fully developed voices, including some individuals in advanced high school groups and the more mature voices found in college choirs, some singers may not be easily paired. Voices which do not blend well because of size, color, or vibrato can be "masked" to a degree by placing them in rows farther back in the section and moving them to outer positions (but not the end) of the rows (4 or 5 in Diagram 34).

The "model pair" matching procedure, like the mixed quartet seating position, is most effective when the singers of the group are of relatively equal ability in singing and musical skills. When the singers' reading and singing skills are uneven, it is advantageous to mix abilities rather than match vocal quality. In this pattern singers with strong voices or strong musical skills are mixed with those of weaker skills and abilities. This allows the weaker singers to hear and "follow" sectional leaders. Since there are usually fewer strong singers than weak, the pattern shown in Diagram 35 may be used to distribute the strength of the section.

DIAGRAM 35

wSw   wSw   wSw

w = weak
S = Strong

EPILOGUE

Conducting cannot be learned by reading a book such as this one. Being a perceptual-motor skill, conducting ultimately must be learned through actual experience on the podium, with a live ensemble, performing real music. Yet conducting, like other skills, requires mastery of technical fundamentals—commonly called "stick technique." Without good technique there can be no real skill. This is one reason why the prose portion of this book was written—to present conducting technique in a logical, sequential fashion, so that acquiring those skills might be accomplished as efficiently as possible. We hope we have assisted both teacher and student in achieving this goal.

In an effort to be practical, the inclusion of chapters on score reading and preparation, plus rehearsal procedure seemed essential. They are an integral part of every conductor's job. Accordingly, we hope that this material provides helpful guidance for young conductors and that experienced conductors and teachers may also find some new ideas worthy of trial.

Part II, Musical Excerpts for the Conducting Class, which follows, is designed for the application of "stick technique," score preparation, and rehearsal procedure. The excerpts are intended to be sufficiently long to allow the conducting student to become involved in the expressive qualities of the music itself. We hope that both teachers and students enjoy using these excerpts.

Conducting: A Comprehensive Bibliography

ADLER, SAMUEL. *Choral Conducting.* Chicago: Holt, Rhinehart and Winston, 1971.

BAKALEINIKOFF, VLADIMIR. *Elementary Rules of Conducting for Orchestra, Band and Chorus.* New York: Belwin, 1938.

BAMBERGER, CARL, ed. *The Conductor's Art.* New York: McGraw-Hill, 1965.

BERLIOZ, HECTOR. *The Conductor.* London: W. Reeves, n.d.

BLACKMAN, CHARLES. *Behind the Baton.* New York: Charos Enterprises, 1964.

BOULT, SIR ADRIAN CEDRIC. *A Handbook on the Technique of Conducting.* Oxford: Hall the Printer, Ltd., 1943. (Revised edition, 1968.)

——. *Thoughts on Conducting.* London: Phoenix House, 1963.

BOWLES, MICHAEL. *The Art of Conducting.* Garden City, NY: Doubleday, 1959.

BRAITHWAITE, WARWICK. *The Conductor's Art.* London: Williams & Norgate, 1952.

BUSCH, BRIAN R. *The Complete Choral Conductor: Gesture and Method.* New York: Schirmer Books, 1984.

CHRISTY, VAN A. *Glee Club and Chorus.* New York: Schirmer, 1940.

COAR, BIRCHARD. *The Masters of the Classical Period as Conductors.* DeKalb, IL: (n.p.), 1949.

COX-IFE, WILLIAM. *The Elements of Conducting.* Foreward by Sir Adrian Boult. New York: J. Day Co., 1964.

DAVISON, ARCHIBALD THOMPSON. *Choral Conducting.* Cambridge, MA: Harvard University Press, 1954.

DECKER, HAROLD A. and JULIUS HERFORD. *Choral Conducting: A Symposium.* New York: Appleton-Century-Crofts, 1973.

DECKER, HAROLD A. and COLLEEN J. KIRK. *Choral Conducting: Focus on Communication.* Englewood Cliffs, NJ: Prentice-Hall, 1988.

DISHINGER, CHRISTIAN. *A Conductor's Daily Warm-Ups.* Lebanon, IN: Studio PR, 1976.

EARHART, WILL. *The Eloquent Baton.* New York: M. Witmark and Sons, 1939.

EHMANN, WILHELM. *Choral Directing.* (Transcribed by George D. Wieke.) Minneapolis, MN: Augsburg Publishing House, 1960.

EHRET, WALTER. *The Choral Conductor's Handbook.* New York: Edward B. Marks Music, 1959.

FINN, WILLIAM J. *The Art of the Choral Conductor,* Vol. 1. Boston: C.C. Birchard, 1940.

————. *The Conductor Raises His Baton*. New York and London: Harper & Brothers, 1944.

FUCHS, PETER PAUL. *The Psychology of Conducting*. New York: MCA Music, 1969.

GARRETSON, ROBERT. *Conducting Choral Music*. Boston: Allyn and Bacon, 1981.

GEHRKENS, KARL WILSON. *Essentials in Conducting*. Boston: Oliver Ditson, 1919.

GILLIS, DON. *The Unfinished Symphony Conductor*. Austin: Pemberton Press, 1967.

GOLDBECK, FREDERIC. *The Perfect Conductor: An Introduction to His Skill and Art for Musicians and Music-Lovers*. New York: Pellegrini and Gadachy, 1951.

GREEN, ELIZABETH A. H. *The Modern Conductor* (4th ed.). Englewood Cliffs, NJ: Prentice-Hall, 1987.

GROSBAYNE, BENJAMIN. *Techniques of Modern Orchestral Conducting* (2nd ed.). Cambridge, MA: Harvard University Press, 1973.

HABERLEN, JOHN BLACK. *Mastering Conducting Techniques*. Champaign, IL: Mark Foster Music, 1977.

HAWKES, FREDERICK G. *Studies in Time and Tempo: A Handbook for Conductors*. London: Salvationist Publications and Supplies, c. 1936.

HEFFERNAN, CHARLES W. *Choral Music: Technique and Artistry*. Englewood Cliffs, NJ: Prentice-Hall, 1982.

HOLMES, MALCOLM H. *Conducting an Amateur Orchestra*. Cambridge, MA: Harvard University Press, 1951.

HUNSBERGER, DONALD and ROY ERNST. *The Art of Conducting*. New York: Alfred A. Knopf, 1983.

INGELBRECHT, DESIRE EMILE. *The Conductor's World*. (Translated from French.) London: P. Nevill, 1953.

JACOBSON, BERNARD. *Conductors on Conducting*. Frenchtown, NJ: Columbia Publishing, 1979.

JONES, ARCHIE NEFF. *Techniques in Choral Conducting*. New York: C. Fischer, 1948.

KAHN, EMIL. *Elements of Conducting* (2nd ed.). New York: Schirmer Books, 1975.

KAPLAN, ABRAHAM. *Choral Conducting*. New York: W. W. Norton, 1985.

KENDRIE, FRANK ESTIES. *Handbook on Conducting and Orchestral Routines*. New York: H. W. Gray, 1930.

KINYON, JOHN LEROY. *The Teacher on the Podium*, Sherman Oaks, CA: Alfred Music, 1975.

KRONE, MAX T. *The Chorus and Its Conductor*. Park Ridge, IL: Neil A. Kjos Music, 1945.

————. *Expressive Conducting*. Chicago: Neil A. Kjos, 1949.

KRUEGER, KARL. *The Way of the Conductor: His Origins, Purpose and Procedures*. New York: Charles Scribner's Sons, 1958.

LABUTA, JOSEPH. *Basic Conducting Technique* (2nd ed.). Englewood Cliffs, NJ: Prentice-Hall, 1989.

LAMB, GORDON H. *Choral Techniques*. Dubuque, IA: William C. Brown, 1974.

LEE, JACK. *Modern Conducting Techniques*. Winona, MN: Hal Leonard Music, 1972.

LEINSDORF, ERICH. *The Composer's Advocate*. New Haven: Yale University Press, 1981.

LEWIS, JOSEPH. *Conducting Without Fears: A Helpful Handbook for the Beginner*. London: Ascherberg, Hopwood and Crew, 1953–55.

LONG, R. GERRY. *The Conductor's Workshop: A Workbook on Instrumental Conducting* (2nd ed.). Dubuque: Wm. C. Brown, 1977.

MCELHERAN, BROCK. *Conducting Techniques for Beginners and Professionals*. New York: Oxford University Press, 1966.

MALKO, NIKOLAI ANDREEVICH. *The Conductor and His Baton: Fundamentals of the Technique of Conducting*. Copenhagen: W. Hansen, 1950.

MARPLE, HUGO DIXON. *The Beginning Conductor*. New York: McGraw-Hill, 1972.

MOSES, DON V, ROBERT W. DEMAREE, JR., and ALLEN F. OHMES. *Face to Face with an Orchestra*. Princeton: Prestige, 1987.

MUNCH, CHARLES. *I Am a Conductor*. (Translated by Leonard Burkat.) New York: Oxford University Press, 1955.

NOYES, FRANK. *Fundamentals of Conducting*. Dubuque, IA: Wm. C. Brown, 1954.

OTTERSTEIN, ADOLPH WM. *The Baton in Motion: A Photographic Presentation of the Technique of Conducting, Together with Materials for Practice*. New York and Boston: Carl Fischer, 1940.

PRAUSNITZ, FREDERICK. *Score and Podium.* New York: W. W. Norton, 1983.

ROSS, ALLAN A. *Techniques for Beginning Conductors.* Belmont, CA: Wadsworth, 1976.

RUDOLF, MAX. The Grammar of Conducting (2nd ed.). New York: Schirmer Books, 1980.

SAMINSKY, LAZARE. *Essentials of Conducting.* London: Dennis Dobson, 1958.

SCHERCHEN, HERMANN. *Handbook of Conducting.* London: Oxford University Press, 1933.

SCHMID, ADOLF. *The Language of the Baton.* New York: G. Schirmer, 1937.

SCHROEDER, CARL. *Handbook of Conducting.* London: Augener, 190-?

STANTON, ROYAL. *The Dynamic Choral Conductor.* Delaware Water Gap, PA: Shawnee Press, 1971.

STOESSEL, ALBERT. *The Technique of the Baton.* New York: Carl Fischer, 1928.

SWIFT, FREDERIC FAY. *Fundamentals of Conducting.* Rockville Centre, NY: Belwin, 1961.

THOMAS, KURT. *The Choral Conductor.* New York: Associated Music Publishers, 1971.

VAN BODEGRAVEN, PAUL. *The School Music Conductor: Problems and Practices in Choral and Instrumental Conducting.* Chicago: Hall-McCleary, 1942.

VAN HOESEN, KARL DUANE. *Handbook for Conducting,* rev. ed. New York: Appleton-Century-Crofts, 1950.

WAGNER, RICHARD. *On Conducting* (2nd ed.). London: W. Reeves, 1897.

WEINGARTNER, FELIX. *On Conducting.* New York: Kalmus, n.d.

WILSON, HARRY R. *A Guide for Choral Conductors.* New York: Silver Burdett, 1950.

WOOD, SIR HENRY JOSEPH. *About Conducting.* London: Sylvan Press, 1945.

TOPICS RELATED TO CONDUCTING

A. General Musical References
B. New Music
C. Score Study and Analysis
D. Musical Form
E. Articulation and Bowing
F. Diction
G. Style and Interpretation
   1. General Texts
   2. Choral Music
   3. Instrumental Music
H. Rehearsal Techniques
I. Performance Techniques
J. Orchestration and Arranging
K. Calligraphy
L. On Orchestras and Their Conductors
M. Music Guides for Band, Choir, and Orchestra

A. *General Musical References*

BUKOFZER, MANFRED F. *Music in the Baroque Era.* New York: W. W. Norton, 1964.

CHASE, GILBERT. *America's Music.* New York: McGraw-Hill, 1955.

GROUT, DONALD JAY. *A History of Western Music* (4th ed.). New York: W. W. Norton, 1988.

PAULY, REINHARD. *Music in the Classic Period* (3rd ed.). Englewood Cliffs, NJ: Prentice-Hall, 1988.

REESE, GUSTAVE. *Music in the Renaissance.* New York: W. W. Norton, 1959.

ULRICH, HOMER. *Symphonic Music.* New York: Columbia University Press, 1952.

B. *New Music*

AUSTIN, WILLIAM A. *Music in the Twentieth Century.* New York: W. W. Norton, 1966.

BARTOLOZZI, BRUNO. *New Sounds for Woodwinds.* (Translated and edited by Reginald Smith Brindle.) London: Oxford University Press, 1967.

CAGE, JOHN. *Notations.* New York: Something Else Press, Inc., 1969.

COPE, DAVID. *New Directions in Music.* New York: W. C. Brown, 1971.

———. *New Music Notation.* Dubuque, IA: Kendall, Hunt Publishing, 1976.

DALLIN, LEON. *Techniques of Twentieth Century Composition.* (3rd ed.). New York: Wm. C. Brown, 1974.

DERI, OTTO. *Exploring Twentieth Century Music.* New York: Holt, Rinehart and Winston, 1968.

DORN, KEN. *Saxophone Technique, Vol. 1: Multiphonics.* Islington, MA: Dorn Productions, 1975.

GRIFFITHS, PAUL. *A Concise History of Avant-Garde Music.* New York: Oxford University Press, 1978.

SALZMAN, ERIC. *Twentieth-Century Music: An Introduction* (3rd ed.). Englewood Cliffs, NJ: Prentice-Hall, 1988.

WILDER, ROBERT D. *Twentieth-Century Music.* Dubuque, IA: Wm. C. Brown, 1969.

C. Score Study and Analysis

BERNSTEIN, MARTIN. *Score Reading.* New York: M. Witmark and Sons, 1947.

COOPER, G. W., and L. B. MEYER. *The Rhythmic Structure of Music.* Chicago: The University of Chicago Press, 1960.

FENNELL, FREDERICK. *Basic Band Repertory.* Evanston: The Instrumentalist, 1980.

FISKE, ROGER. *Score Reading.* 3 vols. London: Oxford University Press, 1958.

GREEN, ELIZABETH A. H. and NICOLAI MALKO. *The Conductor's Score.* (Formerly *The Conductor and His Score.*) Englewood Cliffs, NJ: Prentice-Hall, 1985.

GRUNOW, RICHARD F., and MILFORD H. FARGO. *The Choral Score Reading Program.* Chicago: G.I.A. Publications, 1985.

HUNSBERGER, DONALD. "Score Study and Preparation." *The Instrumentalist,* August 1980, 17–25; September 1980, 34–39.

JACOB, GORDON. *How to Read a Score.* New York: Boosey & Hawkes, 1944.

ROOD, LOUISE. *How to Read a Score.* New York: Edwin Kalmus, 1948.

WALKER, ALAN. *A Study in Musical Analysis.* New York: Free Press, 1963.

D. Musical Form

BERRY, WALLACE. *Form in Music* (2nd ed.). Englewood Cliffs, NJ: Prentice-Hall, 1986.

CONE, EDWARD T. *Musical Form and Musical Performance.* New York: W. W. Norton, 1968.

DAVIE, CEDRIC THORPE. *Musical Structure and Design.* London: Dennis Dobson, 1953.

ESCHMAN, KARL. *Changing Forms in Modern Music.* Boston: E. C. Schirmer, 1945.

FONTAINE, PAUL. *Basic Formal Structure in Music.* New York: Appleton-Century-Crofts, 1967.

GREEN, DOUGLASS. *Form in Tonal Music.* Boston: Holt, Rinehart & Winston, 1966.

READ, GARDNER. *Form and Orchestration.* New York: Schirmer Books, 1980.

STEIN, ERWIN. *Form and Performance.* New York: Alfred A. Knopf, 1952.

STEIN, LEON. *Anthology of Musical Forms.* Evanston: Sunny-Birchard, 1962.

———. *Structure and Style.* Evanston: Sunny-Birchard, 1962.

E. Articulation and Bowing

GREEN, ELIZABETH A. H. *Orchestral Bowing and Routines.* Ann Arbor, MI: Campus Publishers, 1957.

KELLER, HERMANN. *Phrasing and Articulation.* (Chapters 4–6, 8–12.) New York: W. W. Norton, 1965.

KOHUT, DANIEL L., *Instrumental Music Pedagogy.* (Chapter 4.) Englewood Cliffs, NJ: Prentice-Hall, 1973.

LORRIN, MARK. *Dictionary of Bowing and Tonal Techniques for Strings.* Denver: Charles Hansen Educational Music and Books, 1968.

McBeth, W. Francis. *Effective Performance of Band Music,* Solution II. San Antonio: Southern Music, 1972.

Rabin, Marvin, and Priscilla Smith. *Guide to*

Orchestral Bowings Through Musical Styles. Madison: University of Wisconsin Press, Extension Arts, 1984.

F. Diction

Adler, Kurt. *Phonetics and Diction in Singing.* Minneapolis: University of Minnesota Press, 1965.

Arnold, William. *French Diction for Singers and Speakers.* Philadelphia: Oliver Ditson Company, 1912.

Coffin, Berton. *Coffin's Overtones of Bel Canto: Phonetic Basis of Artistic Singing with One Hundred Chromatic Vowel-Chart Exercises.* Metuchen, NJ: Scarecrow Press, 1980.

———. *Phonetic Reading of Songs and Arias.* Metuchen, NJ: Scarecrow Press, 1982.

Corlomi, Evelina. *Singer's Italian.* New York: Schirmer Books, 1960.

Cox, Richard G. *The Singer's Manual of German and French Diction.* New York: Schirmer Books, 1970.

Errole, Ralph. *Italian Diction for Singers.* Boulder, CO: Pruett Press, 1963.

Grubb, Thomas. *Singing in French: A Manual of French Diction and French Vocal Repertoire.* New York: Schirmer Books, 1979.

Halliday, John R. *Diction for Singers.* Provo, UT: Brigham Young University Press, 1970.

Henschel, Sir George. *Articulation in Singing.* London: The John Church Company, 1926.

Hines, Robert S. *Singer's Manual of Latin Diction and Phonetics.* New York: Schirmer Books, 1975.

Jones, Smith, Wallis. *Pronouncing Guide to*

French, German, Italian, Spanish. New York: Carl Fischer, 1955.

Marshall, Madeline. *The Singer's Manual of English Diction.* New York: Schirmer Books, 1953.

Montani, Nicola A. *The Correct Pronunciation of Latin According to Roman Usage.* Philadelphia: The St. Gregory Guild, 1937.

Moriarty, John. *Diction: Italian, Latin, French, German . . . the Sounds and 81 Exercises for Singing Them.* Boston: E.C. Schirmer Music, 1975.

Odom, William. *German for Singers: A Textbook of Diction and Phonetics.* New York: Schirmer Books, 1981.

Pfautsch, Lloyd. *English Diction for Singers.* New York: Lawson-Gould Music, 1971.

Russell, Louis Arthur. *English Diction for Singers and Speakers.* New York: C. H. Ditson, 1905.

Schafer, R. Murray. *When Words Sing.* Scarborough, Ontario: Bernadol Music, 1970.

Uris, Dorothy. *To Sing in English.* New York: Boosey and Hawkes, 1971.

Waring, Fred. *Tone Syllables.* Delaware Water Gap, PA: Shawnee Press, 1951.

Wierenga, Leanne. *French Diction for the Singer.* New York: Kenyon Publications, 1977.

Wilke, Eva. *German Diction in Singing.* New York: E. P. Dutton, 1930.

G. Style and Interpretation

1. General Texts

Aldrich, Putnam C. *The "Authentic" Performance of Baroque Music: Essays on Music in Honor of Archibald T. Davison.* Cambridge, MA: Harvard University Press, 1957.

Barra, Donald. *The Dynamic Performance: A Performer's Guide to Musical Expression*

and Interpretation. Englewood Cliffs, NJ: Prentice-Hall, 1983.

Crocker, Richard L. *A History of Musical Style.* New York: McGraw-Hill, 1966.

Dart, Thurston. *The Interpretation of Music.* London: Hutchinson's University Library, 1954.

DOLMETSCH, RUDOLPH. *The Interpretation of the Music of the XVII and XVIII Centuries.* London: Novello, 1946.

DONINGTON, ROBERT. *The Interpretation of Music.* London: Faber and Faber, 1963.

DORIAN, FREDERICK. *The History of Music in Performance.* New York: W. W. Norton, 1942.

FISHBACK, HORACE, III. *A Handbook of Musical Style.* Teaneck, NJ: Fairleigh Dickinson University, 1966.

KELLER, HERMANN. *Phrasing and Interpretation.* (Tr. Leigh Gerdine.) New York: W. W. Norton, 1965.

MATTHAY, TOBIAS. *Musical Interpretation.* Boston: Boston Music, 1913.

MOORE, DOUGLAS. *A Guide to Musical Styles.* New York: W.W. Norton, 1962.

SCHOENBERG, ARNOLD. *Style and Idea.* New York: Philosophical Library, 1950.

TARTINI, GUISEPPE. *Treatise on the Ornaments of Music.* (Tr. Sol Babitz.) New York: Carl Fischer, 1956.

THURMOND, JAMES MORGAN. *Note Grouping: A Method for Achieving Expression and Style in Musical Performance.* JMT Publications, P.O. Box 603, Camp Hill, PA 17011.

ULRICH, HOMER. *A History of Music and Musical Style.* New York: Harcourt, Brace & World, 1963.

VAN ESS, DONALD H. *The Heritage of Musical Styles.* New York: Holt, Rinehart and Winston, 1970.

2. Choral Music

ANDREWS, H. K. *The Technique of Byrd's Vocal Polyphony.* London: Oxford University Press, 1966.

APEL, WILLI. *The Notation of Polyphonic Music 900 to 1600.* Cambridge, MA: The Medieval Academy of America, 1953.

CAIN, NOBLE. *Choral Music and Its Practice.* New York: M. Witmark & Sons, 1942.

COWARD, HENRY. *Choral Technique and Interpretation.* London: Novello, n.d.

CRIST, BAINBRIDGE. *The Art of Setting Words to Music.* New York: Carl Fischer, 1944.

DAY, JAMES. *The Literary Background to Bach's Cantatas.* London, Dennis Dobson, 1961.

EINSTEIN, ALFRED. *The Italian Madrigal.* (3 vols.) Princeton, NJ: Princeton University Press, 1949.

FELLOWES, EDMUND HORACE. *The English Madrigal.* London: Oxford University Press, 1925.

GARRETSON, ROBERT L. *Conducting Choral Music.* Boston: Allyn and Bacon, 1975.

HAAR, JAMES. *Chanson and Madrigal.* Cambridge, MA: Harvard University Press, 1964.

HOWERTON, GEORGE. *Technique and Style in Choral Singing.* New York: Carl Fischer, 1957.

JACOBS, ARTHUR, ed. *Choral Music: A Symposium.* Baltimore, MD: Penguin Books, 1963.

KERMAN, JOSEPH. *The Elizabethan Madrigal.* New York: Galaxy Music Corporation, distributor for American Musicological Society, 1962.

ROBINSON, RAY, and ALLEN WINOLD. *The Choral Experience.* New York: Harper and Row, 1976.

ROCHE, JEROME. *The Madrigal.* New York: Charles Scribner's Sons, 1972.

SCOTT, CHARLES KENNEDY. *Madrigal Singing.* London: Oxford University Press, 1931.

TERRY, CHARLES SANFORD. *Joh. Seb. Bach Cantata Texts, Sacred and Secular.* London: Constable, 1926.

TUFTS, NANCY POORE. *The Children's Choir* (Vol. II). Philadelphia, PA: Fortress Press, 1965.

ULRICH, HOMER. *A Survey of Choral Music.* Chicago: Harcourt Brace Jovanovich, 1973.

YOUNG, PERCEY M. *The Choral Tradition.* London: Hutchinson, 1962.

3. Instrumental Music

ADKINS, HECTOR ERNEST. *Treatise on the Military Band* (2nd rev. ed.). London: Boosey and Hawkes, 1958.

BERG, DAVID ERIC. *Early and Classic Symphonies and the Functions of a Conductor.* New York: The Caxton Institute, 1927.

GOLDMAN, ORCHARD FRANKO. *The Wind Band, Its Literature and Technique.* Boston: Allyn and Bacon, 1962.

WEINGARTNER, FELIX. *On the Performance of the Beethoven Symphonies.* (Tr. Jessie Crosland.) New York: Edwin F. Kalmus, n.d.

H. Rehearsal Techniques

BOYD, JACK. *Rehearsal Guide for the Choral Direc-tor.* West Nyack, NY: Parker, 1971.

HOVEY, NILO. *Efficient Rehearsal Procedures for School Bands.* Elkhart, IN: Selmer, 1976.

HOWERTON, GEORGE. *Technique and Style in Cho-ral Singing.* New York: Carl Fisher, 1957.

GREEN, ELIZABETH A. H. *The Dynamic Orchestra: Principles of Orchestral Performance for In-strumentalists, Conductors and Audiences.* Englewood Cliffs, NJ: Prentice-Hall, 1987.

KOHUT, DANIEL L. *Instrumental Music Pedagogy.*

(Chapter 8.) Englewood Cliffs, NJ: Prentice-Hall, 1973.

LONG, R. GERRY. *The Conductor's Workshop*, Part I. Dubuque, IA: Wm. C. Brown, 1977.

NEIDIG, KENNETH and JOHN, JENNINGS. *Choral Director's Guide.* West Nyack, NY: Parker, 1967.

ROE, PAUL F. *Choral Music Education.* Englewood Cliffs, NJ: Prentice-Hall, 1970.

ROTHROCK, CARSON. *Training the High School Or-chestra.* New Nyack, NY: Parker, 1971.

I. Performance Techniques

1. Instrumental

COLWELL, RICHARD J. *The Teaching of Instrumen-tal Music.* New York: Appleton-Century-Crofts, 1969.

GREEN, ELIZABETH A. H. *Teaching Stringed Instru-ments in Classes.* Englewood Cliffs, NJ: Prentice-Hall, 1966.

HUNT, NORMAN J. *Guide to Teaching Brass Instru-ments.* Dubuque, IA: Wm. C. Brown, 1968.

KOHUT, DANIEL L. *Instrumental Music Pedagogy: Teaching Techniques for School Band and Orchestra Directors.* Englewood Cliffs, NJ: Prentice-Hall, 1973.

PAYSON, AL and JACK MCKENZIE. *Music Educator's Guide to Percussion.* New York: Belwin, 1966.

WESTPHAL, FREDERICK W. *Guide to Teaching Woodwinds: Flute, Oboe, Clarinet, Bassoon, Saxophone.* Dubuque, IA: Wm. C. Brown, 1962.

2. Choral

ALDERSON, RICHARD. *Complete Handbook of Voice Training.* West Nyack, NY: Parker, 1979.

APPELMAN, RALPH. *The Science of Vocal Pedagogy.* Bloomington: Indiana University Press, 1967.

ARMSTRONG, KERCHAL, and DONALD HUSTAD. *Cho-ral Musicianship and Voice Training: An In-troduction.* Carol Stream, IL: Somerset Press, 1986.

CHRISTY, VAN A. *Expressive Singing.* Dubuque, IA: W. C. Brown, 1961.

EHMAN, WILHELM, and FRANKE HAASEMANN. *Voice Building for Choirs.* Chapel Hill, NC: Hin-shaw Music, 1982.

MILLER, RICHARD. *The Structure of Singing.* New York: Schirmer Books, 1986.

REID, CORNELIUS L. *The Free Voice: A Guide to Natural Singing.* New York: Coleman-Ross, 1965.

TRUSLER, IVAN and WALTER EHRET. *Functional Lessons in Singing* (2nd ed.). Englewood Cliffs, NJ: Prentice-Hall, 1972.

VENNARD, WILLIAM. *Singing: The Mechanism and the Technic.* Rev. ed. New York: C. Fischer, 1967.

J. Orchestration and Arranging (Including Choral)

ADES, HAWLEY. *Choral Arranging.* Delaware Water Gap, PA: Shawnee Press, 1966.

ADLER, SAMUEL. *The Study of Orchestration.* New York: W. W. Norton, 1982.

BAKER, MICKEY. *Complete Handbook for the Music Arranger.* New York: Amsco, 1970.

BENNETT, ROBERT RUSSELL. *Instrumentally Speak-ing.* Melville, NY: Belwin-Mills, 1975.

BERLIOZ, HECTOR. *Treatise on Instrumentation.* (Enlarged and revised by Richard Strauss; tr. Theodore Front.) New York: E. F. Kalmus, 1948.

BLATTER, ALFRED. *Instrumentation/Orchestration.* New York: Longman, 1980.

CACAVAS, JOHN. *Music Arranging and Orchestration.* Melville, NY: Belwin-Mills, 1975.

CARSE, ADAM. *The History of Orchestration.* New York: Dover, 1964.

COLLINSON, FRANCIS M. *Orchestration for the Theatre.* London: John Lane, 1949.

DAVISON, ARCHIBALD T. *The Technique of Choral Composition.* Cambridge, MA: Harvard University Press, 1945.

FORSYTH, CECIL. *Orchestration* (2nd ed.). New York: Macmillan, 1942.

GARDNER, MAURICE. *The Orchestrator's Handbook.* New York: Staff Music, 1972.

ISSAC, MERLE J. *Practical Orchestration.* New York: Robbins Music, 1963.

JACOB, GORDON. *The Elements of Orchestration.* New York: October House, 1962.

———. *Orchestral Technique.* London: Oxford University Press, 1940.

KENNEN, KENT and DONALD GRANTHAM. *The Technique of Orchestration* (4th ed.). Englewood Cliffs, NJ: Prentice-Hall, 1990.

———. *Orchestration Workbook.* New York: Prentice-Hall, 1969.

LANG, PHILIP. *Scoring for the Band.* New York: Mills Music, 1950.

LEIDZEN, ERICK. *An Invitation to Band Arranging.* Philadelphia: Oliver Ditson, 1950.

MCKAY, GEORGE FREDERICK. *Creative Orchestration* (2nd ed.). Boston: Allyn and Bacon, 1969.

MERRILL, BARZILLE WINFRED. *Practical Introduction to Orchestration and Instrumentation.* Ann Arbor, MI: Edwards Brothers, 1937.

PARROTT, IAN. *Method in Orchestration.* London: Dobson, 1957.

PISTON, WALTER. *Orchestration.* New York: W. W. Norton, 1955.

RAUSCHER, DONALD J. *Orchestration Scores and Scoring.* New York: Free Press of Glencoe, 1963.

RIMSKI-KORSAKOV, NIKOLAI. *Principles of Orchestration.* (Ed. Maximilian Steinberg; tr. Edward Agate.) New York: Dover, 1964.

ROGERS, BERNARD. *The Art of Orchestration.* New York: Appleton-Century-Crofts, 1951.

SEBESKY, DON. *The Contemporary Arranger.* New York: Alfred Music, 1975.

WAGNER, JOSEPH. *Band Scoring.* New York: McGraw-Hill, 1960.

———. *Orchestration: A Practical Handbook.* New York: McGraw-Hill, 1959.

WILSON, HARRY ROBERT. *Choral Arranging.* New York: Robbins Music, 1949.

K. Calligraphy

HEUSSENSTAMM, GEORGE. *The Norton Manual of Music Notation.* New York: W. W. Norton, 1987.

READ, GARDNER. *Music Notation: A Manual of Modern Practice.* Boston: Allyn and Bacon, Inc., 1969.

L. On Orchestras and Their Conductors

American Symphony Orchestra League. *A Report on Conductor Study and Training Opportunities.* Helen W. Thompson, Exec. Sec., Charleston, West Virginia, 1960.

ANTEK, SAMUEL. *This Was Toscanini.* New York: Vanguard Press, 1963.

CARSE, ADAM VON AHN. *The Orchestra from Beethoven to Berlioz: A History of the Orchestra in the First Half of the 19th Century; and of the Development of Orchestral Baton Conducting.* New York: Broude Brothers, 1949.

EWEN, DAVID. *Dictators of the Baton* (2nd ed.). Chicago: Ziff-Davis, 1948.

———. *The Man with the Baton: The Story of Conductors and Their Orchestras.* New York: Thomas Y. Crowell, 1936.

HUGHES, PATRICK CAIRNS. *The Toscanini Legacy: A Critical Study of Arturo Toscanini's Performances of Beethoven, Verdi and Other Composers* (2nd ed.). New York: Dover, 1969.

SCHONBERG, HAROLD C. *The Great Conductors.* New York: Simon and Schuster, 1967.

WALTER, BRUNO. *Of Music and Music-Making.* (Tr. Paul Hamburger.) New York: W. W. Norton, 1961.

M. Music Guides for Band, Choir, and Orchestra

ASCAP Symphonic Catalogue (3rd ed.). American Society of Composers, Authors, and Publishers. New York: R. R. Bowker, 1977.

Band Music Guide. Evanston, IL: The Instrumentalist, 1982.

BURNSWORTH, CHARLES C. *Choral Music for Women's Voices.* Metuchen, NJ: Scarecrow Press, 1968.

Catalogue of Orchestral Music. Sydney: Australia Music Centre, 1976.

Contemporary Music: A Suggested List for High Schools and Colleges. Washington, DC: MENC, 1964.

DANIELS, DAVID. *Orchestral Music: A Handbook* (2nd ed.). Metuchen, NJ: Scarecrow Press, 1982.

DVORAK, THOMAS L. *Best Music For Young Band.* Brooklyn, NY: Manhattan Beach Music, 1986.

FARISH, MARGARET K. *Orchestral Music in Print* (1st ed.). Philadelphia: Musicdata, 1979.

FITTS, MURIEL. *String Orchestra List, Graded and Selected: Easy, Intermediate, Advanced.* ASTA (available from Theodore Presser, Bryn Mawr, PA).

HAWKINS, MARGARET. *An Annotated Inventory of Distinctive Choral Literature for Performance at the High School Level.* Tampa, FL: American Choral Directors Association, 1976.

JACOBS, ARTHUR. *Choral Music: A Symposium.* Baltimore, MD: Penguin Books, 1963.

KJELSON, LEE and JAMES MCCRAY. *The Conductor's Manual of Choral Music Literature.* Melville, NY: Belwin-Mills, 1973.

LASTER, JAMES. *Catalogue of Choral Music Arranged in Biblical Order.* Metuchen, NJ: Scarecrow Press, 1983.

LOCKE, ARTHUR W., and CHARLES K. FASSETT, compilers. *Selected List of Choruses for Women's Voices.* Northampton, MA: Smith College, 1964.

MATESKY, RALPH. *Compendium of Recommended School Orchestra Literature.* ASTA (available from Theodore Presser, Bryn Mawr, PA).

Military and Brass Band Music. Sydney: Australia Music Centre, 1977.

NARDONE, THOMAS R. *Choral Music in Print.* Philadelphia: Musicdata, 1974.

Orchestra Music Guide. Evanston: The Instrumentalist, 1966.

ROACH, DONALD W., project coordinator. *Music for Children's Choirs: A Selected and Graded Listing.* Reston, VA: Music Educators National Conference, 1977.

Selected Music Lists: Chorus, Orchestra, String Orchestra and Band. Washington, DC: Music Educators National Conference, 1971.

Selected Music Lists–1978: Full Orchestra, String Orchestra. Reston, VA: Music Educator's National Conference (c. 1978).

SHERMAN, HAL. *Techniques and Materials for Stage Band.* Los Angeles: Creative World Music Publications (n.d.).

TORTOLANO, WILLIAM. *Original Music for Men's Voices: A Selected Bibliography* (2nd ed.). Metuchen, NJ: Scarecrow Press, 1981.

Vocal and Choral Music. Sydney: Australia Music Centre, 1976.

WHITE, EVELYN DAVIDSON. *Choral Music by Afro-American Composers: A Selected, Annotated Bibliography.* Metuchen, NJ: Scarecrow Press, 1981.

YOUNG, ALLEN. *Choral Educators Resource Handbook.* San Francisco: Choral Resource Seminars, 1985.

Musical Excerpts for the Conducting Class

ALPHABETICAL LISTING BY COMPOSER

*This symbol indicates that the work is designed to be performed by both choral and instrumental ensembles.

*BACH, JOHANN SEBASTIAN. *Hail to Thee Jesus Kind.*

BANCHIERI, ADRIANO. Sinfonia.

BEETHOVEN, LUDWIG VAN. Symphony No. 5, opening section.

*BILLINGS, WILLIAM. *Chester.*

BIZET, GEORGES. Symphony No. 1 in C, second movement.

BRAHMS, JOHANNES. "How Lovely is Thy Dwelling Place," from *A German Requiem,* movement four.

*BURT, ALFRED. *Christ in the Stranger's Guise.*

DVŎŘAK, ANTONIN. Slovanic Dance, Op. 46, No. 1.

ELGAR, EDWARD. "Nimrod" from *Enigma Variations.*

GRIEG, EDVARD. "Ase's Death" from *Peer Gynt.*

HOLST, GUSTAV. Second Suite in F for Military Band.
   March, opening section.
   March, measures 43–78.

*McKELVEY, JAMES. *Deck the Halls (in 7/8).*

MOUSSORGSKY, MODEST. "Promenade" from *Pictures at an Exhibition.*

*PATRIOTIC. *America.*
   Star-Spangled Banner.

RIMSKY-KORSAKOFF, NICOLAI. *Scheherazade.*

ROSSINI, GIOACCHINO. Overture to *The Italian Girl in Algiers.*

SCHUBERT, FRANZ. Kyrie from *Mass in G.*
   Sanctus, from *Mass in C.*

STRAVINSKY, IGOR. Finale, from *Firebird* Suite.
   Petroushka.

TCHAIKOWSKY, PETER ILLICH. Symphony No. 6.
   Main theme, first movement.
   Theme from second movement.

THOMPSON, RANDALL. *Glory to God in the Highest.*

*TRADITIONAL. *Londonderry Air.*

VIVALDI, ANTONIO. *Gloria,* second movement.

WAGNER, RICHARD. Prelude to *Die Meistersinger.*

WASHBURN, ROBERT. "Voyager's Song," from *Three Thoughts from Thoreau.*

LISTED BY ORDER OF DIFFICULTY

America. Legato three pattern; good first conducting piece.

Wagner's Prelude to *Die Meistersinger.* Marcato four pattern. Be sure to give a solid ictus on beat three of measure two, six, and similar measures to ensure that the eighth notes following the tie are played aggressively and on time. Player tendency will be to hesitate and play them late.

Billings' *Chester.* This relatively simple piece is the first introduction to the melded gesture. Half and whole notes, when appearing in all parts, should be melded. TEXT REFERENCE: page 45.

Holst's Second Suite, opening of the March. Uses two types of the two pattern: (1) passive beat two, and (2) active beat two. TEXT REFERENCE: page 24.

Rossini's Overture to *The Italian Girl in Algiers.* Light, slow staccato three pattern. TEXT REFERENCE: page 33. Don't conduct beat three. Accents. TEXT REFERENCE: page 39.

Dvořak's Slovanic Dance, Op. 46, No. 1. Three-four meter conducted in one. TEXT REFERENCE: page 27. Introduction to the "no break" fermata. TEXT REFERENCE: page 52. Heavy staccato and legato style contrasts. TEXT REFERENCE: page 32.

Holst's Second Suite, measures 43–78 of the March. Opens with a four-measure diminuendo. TEXT REFERENCE: page 38. Uses fast legato two pattern. TEXT REFERENCE: page 24. Melded gesture used at ends of phrases. TEXT REFERENCE: page 45. Phrase release used at the end of each eighth measure of the solo. TEXT REFERENCE: page 52.

Vivaldi's *Gloria,* second movement. Slow three pattern. First introduction to cuing. TEXT REFERENCE: pages 40 and 44.

Burt's *Christ in the Stranger's Guise.* Uses the six pattern. TEXT REFERENCE: page 62. Starts on beat six. TEXT REFERENCE: page 47. (Executed like an attack on beat four.) Long crescendo. TEXT REFERENCE: page 38. Ritardando. TEXT REFERENCE: page 40. Fermatas on beat four. TEXT REFERENCE: page 52.

Londonderry Air. Starts on beat two in 4/4 meter. TEXT REFERENCE: page 47. Requires indication of breath releases. TEXT REFERENCE: page 52. Rubato/espressivo style including crescendo and decrescendo.

Rimsky-Korsakoff's *Scheherazade.* Slow legato two pattern in 6/8 meter; fractional beat pickup. TEXT REFERENCE: page 48. Espressivo style including crescendo and decrescendo. TEXT REFERENCE: page 38.

Banchieri's Sinfonia. In 4/4 meter. Contrapuntal work in five voices with main focus on cuing. TEXT REFERENCE: page 40 and 44.

Brahms' "How Lovely is Thy Dwelling Place" from *A German Requiem.* Melded gestures. TEXT REFERENCE: page 45. Weighted gestures. TEXT REFERENCE: pages 33 and 67.

Bach's *Hail to Thee Jesus Kind.* Contains fermatas on every beat in 4/4 meter. TEXT REFERENCE: page 52.

Tchaikowsky's Symphony No. 6, first movement. Starts on "and" after beat three in 4/4 meter. TEXT REFERENCE: page 48. Frequent use of crescendo and decrescendo. TEXT REFERENCE: pages 38.

Schubert's Kyrie from Mass in G. Legato three pattern. Weighted gesture. TEXT REFERENCE: page 33 and 67.

Star-Spangled Banner. Starts on beat three in 3/4 meter. TEXT REFERENCE: 47. Fermatas used near the end. TEXT REFERENCE: page 52.

Schubert's Sanctus from Mass in C, fourth movement. Divided four pattern. TEXT REFERENCE: page 62.

Tchaikowsky's Symphony No. 6, second movement. Is in slow 5/4 meter in alternating 3 + 2 and 2 + 3. TEXT REFERENCE: page 56.

Elgar's "Nimrod" from *Enigma Variations.* Weighted gesture. TEXT REFERENCE: page 67. Rubato/espressivo throughout. Must decide where to phrase (take breaths) or if to perform without any breaks.

Beethoven's Symphony No. 5, opening section. Numerous fermatas. TEXT REFERENCE: page 52. 2/4 meter conducted in one. TEXT REFERENCE: page 27. Accents. TEXT REFERENCE: page 39.

Bizet's Symphony No. 1 in C, second movement. Divided three pattern in compound meter (9/8). TEXT REFERENCE: page 63. Dead beats. TEXT REFERENCE: page 46. Espressivo style.

McKelvey's *Deck the Halls*. Asymmetric meter (7/8 conducted in three). TEXT REFERENCE: page 58.

Grieg's "Ase's Death" from *Peer Gynt*. Slow weighted and melded gestures. TEXT REFERENCE: page 67. Divided four pattern may be used, especially when eighth notes predominate.

Robert Washburn's "Voyager's Song" from *Three Thoughts from Thoreau*. Asymmetric meter (7/8 conducted in three) plus rapid changing meters. TEXT REFERENCE: pages 58 and 59.

Stravinsky's Finale from *Firebird* Suite. Uses the seven pattern. TEXT REFERENCE: page 57.

Moussorgsky's "Promenade" from *Pictures at an Exhibition*. Uses changing meters (5/4, 6/4, and 3/2) at a medium tempo. TEXT REFERENCE: pages 56, 62, and 23.

Thompson's *Glory to God in the Highest*. Uses accents. TEXT REFERENCE: page 39. Contains changing meters which alternate from 2/4 to 3/8 to 2/4 to 5/8 etc. TEXT REFERENCE: page 59.

Stravinsky's *Petroushka*. Very challenging and rapid meter changes. TEXT REFERENCE: page 59. Measure 14: beat in one. Measures 15 and 16: combine into one measure and beat in three. All 5/8 measures: beat in one. Treat 4/8 measures as if written in 2/4 meter, i.e. beat in two.

America

Moderato

Patriotic
Arr. Kohut

Overture to *Die Meistersinger*

Richard Wagner

tacet to the end.

Chester

William Billings
Arr. Kohut

Second Suite in F, Opening of the March

Gustave Holst

Overture to *The Italian Girl in Algiers*

Gioacchino Rossini

Slovanic Dance, Op. 46, No. 1

Antonin Dvořák

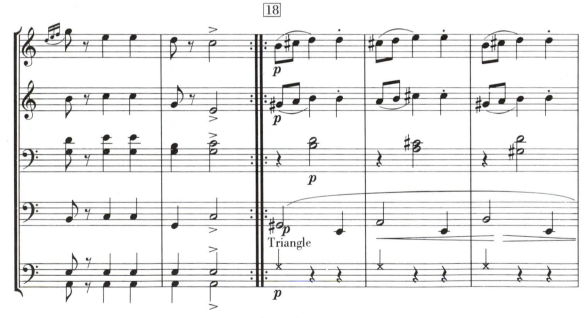

Second Suite in F, meas. 43 - 78 of the March

Gustave Holst

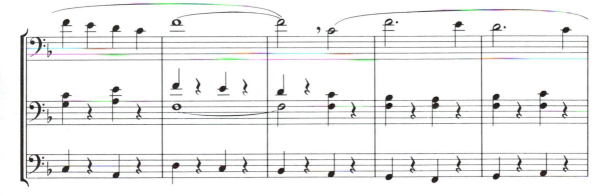

Et in terra pax
(Movement II, *Gloria*)

Antonio Vivaldi
Arr. Grant

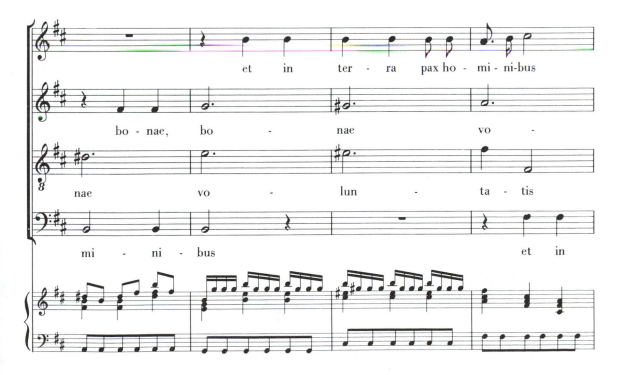

Christ in the Stranger's Guise

Words and Music by
Alfred Burt

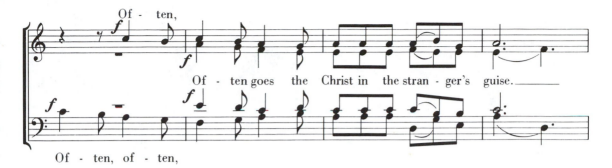

Londonderry Air

Words by Thomas Moore

Traditional Irish
Arr. Kohut

Part III of *Scheherazade*

Andantino quasi Allegretto (♩.= 52)

Nicolai Rimsky-Korsakoff

Sinfonia

Adriano Banchieri

Allegro

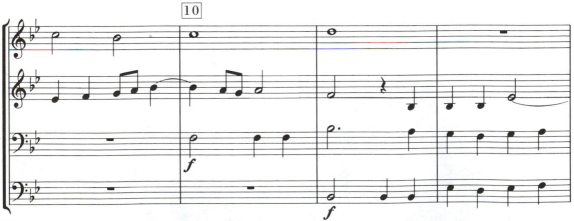

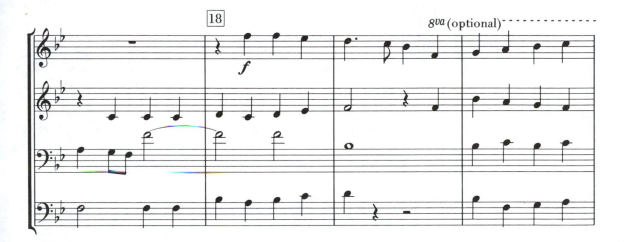

How Lovely Is Thy Dwelling Place
(*A German Requiem*, Op. 45, Mvt. IV)

Johannes Brahms

Hail to Thee, Jesus Kind

Johann Sebastian Bach

Symphony No. 6, 1st Mvt.

Peter Illich Tchaikowsky

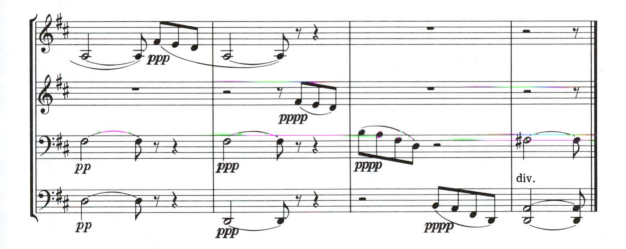

Kyrie
(Mass in G)

Franz Schubert

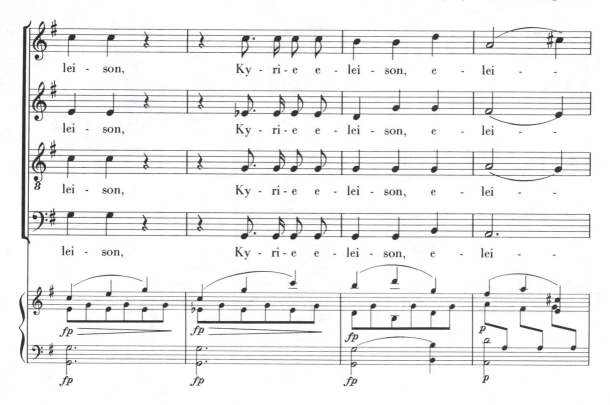

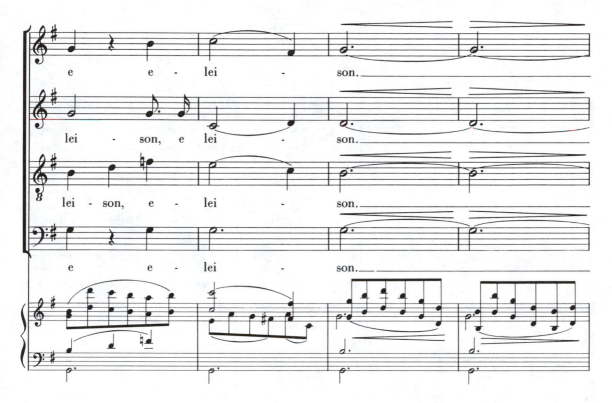

Star-Spangled Banner

Words by Francis Scott Key

stars through the pe-ri-lous fight, o'r the ram-parts we watch'd were so

stars through the pe-ri-lous fight, o'r the ram-parts we watch'd were so

stars through the pe-ri-lous fight, o'r the ram-parts we watch'd were so

stars through the pe-ri-lous fight, o'r the ram-parts we____ watch'd were so

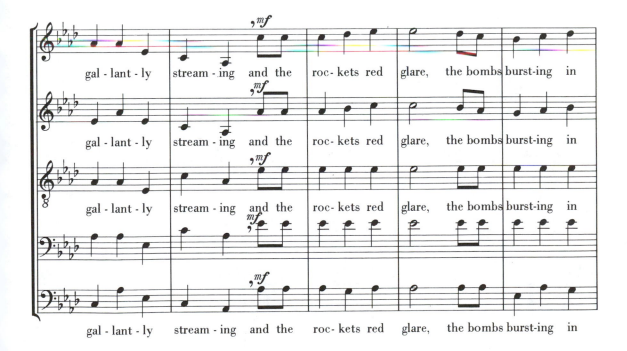

gal-lant-ly stream-ing and the roc-kets red glare, the bombs burst-ing in

gal-lant-ly stream-ing and the roc-kets red glare, the bombs burst-ing in

gal-lant-ly stream-ing and the roc-kets red glare, the bombs burst-ing in

gal-lant-ly stream-ing and the roc-kets red glare, the bombs burst-ing in

Sanctus
(Mass in G)

Franz Schubert

Allegro Maestoso

Symphony No. 6, 2nd Mvt.

Peter Illich Tchaikowsky

Allegro con grazia (♩ = 144)

"Nimrod" from *Enigma Variations*, Op. 36

Edward Elgar

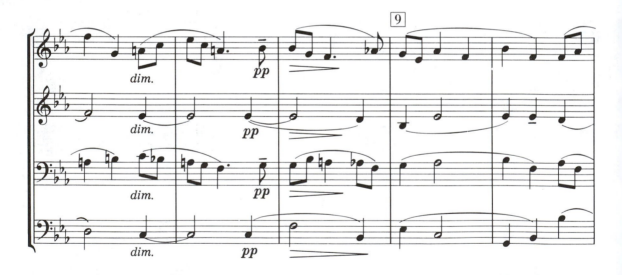

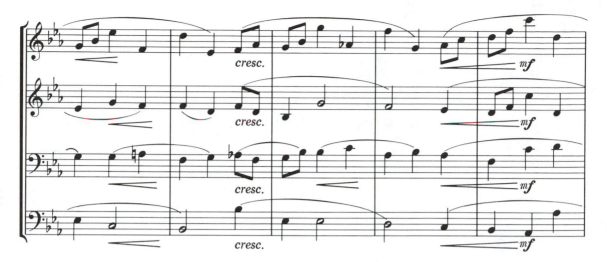

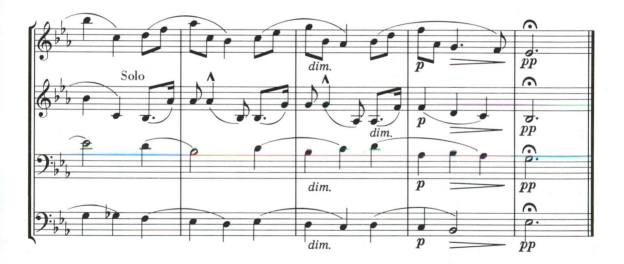

Symphony No. 5

Ludwig van Beethoven

Allegro con brio

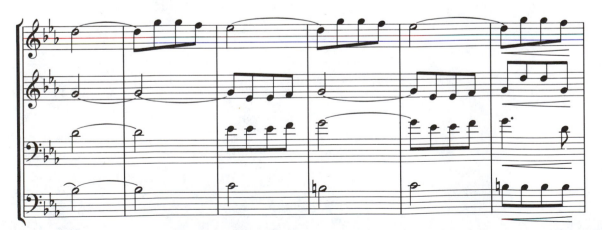

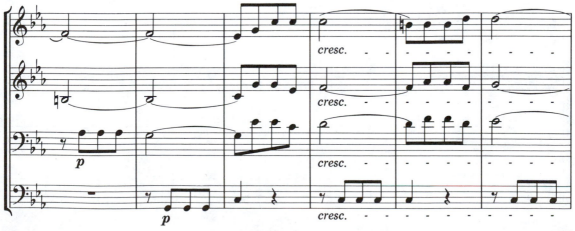

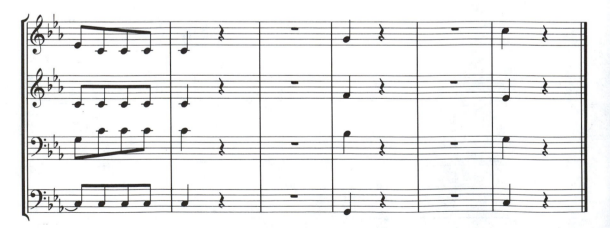

Symphony No. 1 in C, 2nd Mvt.

Georges Bizet

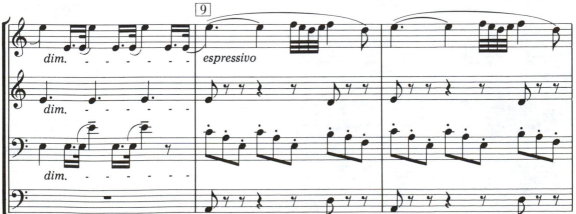

Deck the Halls

Arr. James McKelvy

la   la la . . . .   Fa la la . . . .

"Ase's Death" from *Peer Gynt*, Op. 46, No. 2

Edvard Grieg

Andante doloroso (♩ = 50)

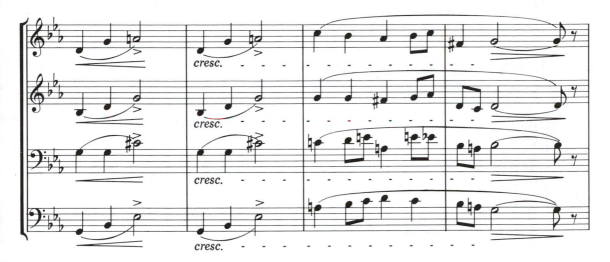

III. Voyager's Song
from *Three Thoughts from Thoreau*

Henry David Thoreau

Robert Washburn

Finale from
The Firebird Suite

Igol Stravinsky

Poco a poco allargando

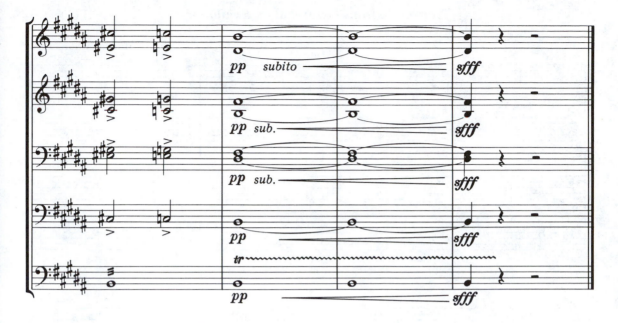

Promenade from *Pictures at an Exhibition*

Allegro   Modest Moussorgsky

Glory to God in the Highest

Petroushka

Igol Stravinsky

Index